DON'T LOOK AT ME IN THAT TONE OF VOICE

(The confusing memories of a sixties childhood)

By

Alex Cotton

For My Amazing Daughter

Kerry

Who Made Me Write This

(Any complaints should be sent to her)

CHAPTER ONE

Call the Dog I'm Here

I was a blue baby. Not in the pissed off sense (that would come later). No, I mean blue because before I could put in an appearance my mother attempted to strangle me with my own umbilical cord. Should have taken that as a warning really.

I was born in the front bedroom of our terraced house in a small street opposite the engineering factory. It was the wee small hours of the morning in early December 1960 and there was thick snow everywhere when my mother went into labour. In a blind panic my father grabbed his pushbike and headed off to the nearest phone box to call for the midwife. Then he took off across the playground up the street to fetch his sister (my Auntie Dolly) for morale support. Such was his panic that he forgot to actually get on his bike and his footprints could clearly be seen in the deep snow running alongside his tyre tracks, bless him.

Anyway, he and my Auntie Dolly made it back to the house and the midwife duly arrived to save my life. After I had been disentangled from my noose and cleaned up, the dog was called up from downstairs to give me a good sniff. Apparently, this was done all the time in those days but I have yet to meet anyone else my age who was sniffed by a dog minutes after entering the world. Maybe this was plan B after the attempted strangling went wrong, either way the dog decided not to eat me and so began my life.

I should add at this point that until I was well into my teenage years I was convinced that I was adopted. My Aunty Dolly would say this couldn't be true as she was there in the room when I was born. I would argue that she had no proof that I was that baby, my mother could have switched babies outside of the shops during one of her 'special' days. Nowadays I have to admit that my Aunty Dolly was right. When I look in the mirror now I can see my brother staring back at me wearing makeup and a wig, and I know he definitely wasn't adopted.

I don't recall much of my first few years, early photos show an average size baby at first. Later ones show a rather plump (obese) child with a round face (three chins) and rosy red cheeks (high blood pressure). Put it this way, I didn't look hungry. Up until the age of five I seem to have been a happy child, I am pictured riding tricycles, pushing dolls in prams, playing the piano (well a small wooden pink one) and running around the park in a very fetching swimming costume with a skirt and frilly knickers attached. It's a good job I didn't take up swimming until I was older, I probably would have drowned wearing that lot. (Aha, that could be plan C).

Anyway, if the photos are to be believed it looks like a happy few years with no sign of the madness (and the fashions) to come.

We lived next door to my nanna (my dad's mother). She idolised my dad and had never forgiven my mother (the evil witch) who had stolen her little boy away from her. When my parents were first married they had lived with my nanna, that was until the man next door gassed himself to death and his house became vacant. They quickly packed up their few belongings and moved in, after making sure the gas board had declared it safe to breathe. I think my mother came to deeply regret living so close to my nanna. Over the years I heard many muffled insults coming over the backyard wall while I was sitting on the outside toilet between the tin bath and the coalhouse.

This only last a few years in any case. When I was around five it was decided that my nanna could no longer manage to get around in her own house anymore and she was duly dispatched to a flat two bus rides away. Even at my tender age I remember being puzzled by the fact that there were two flights of stairs leading up to her flat, more than she had in the house that she could no longer get around in. I think this may have been one of my mother's cunning plans.

After she had moved we would go and visit my nanna every Saturday afternoon and she would take me shopping with her. We were great pals me and my nanna, she didn't like anyone except my older cousin Malcom, my dad and me. We were all in her gang and we could have anything we wanted. I spent many a happy hour parading around her bedroom wearing her hats and jewellery and stuffing my face with all the secret sweets she would buy me, I suppose this could explain the three chins and the rosy red cheeks.

I do recall around that time crying and pleading with my mother to let Nanna come and live with us but to no avail. She was allowed to visit us at Christmas but she was made to sit in the horrible hard chair from upstairs as my mother said she smelt of wee. I really missed having her next door.

Nanna moved away just as I was getting ready to start school, photos from this time show me looking much slimmer. I suppose that could have had something to do with her moving away, I only got to stuff my face on a Saturday now. Also, something strange was starting to happen to my hair. It had always been quite curly and I wore it tied up in a big ribbon, now it seemed to be much shorter and festooned with countless hairgrips. Whenever I quizzed my mother about the hairgrips she would say she was trying to encourage waves. I could never understand why anyone would want to wave to someone with such stupid hair.

When I was eight years old I got my first taste of tragedy, my nanna died suddenly from a brain haemorrhage, leaving me heartbroken. She died while my mother was seven months pregnant with my brother so she never got to see her new grandson. Never mind, she wouldn't have liked him anyway, she'd already told me that whatever my mother produced it wasn't allowed in our gang. RIP Nanna.

CHAPTER TWO

Say Hello to Mrs PMS

Before we go any further I really must introduce you to my mother. Today she is a quite mellow almost eighty-year old tottering around on her walking frame and eating far too many cream buns. This is a bit different to the woman I spent my childhood with. If you ask her today she will tell you that in her day there was no such thing as PMS and it's a new modern thing. I beg to differ here, this woman could have been the poster girl for PMS. For a few weeks at a time we would totter along quite normally (for our family). Then, when you were least expecting it you would be confronted by a snarling, spitting, red eyed she devil across the breakfast table.

She will also tell you nowadays that she cannot bear foul language and that she has never used any bad swear words in her life. Again, I beg to differ, the swearing that came out of that woman was amazing. I had never heard words like that before anywhere else and until I was older and a bit more worldly-wise I thought she must be making them all up.

She also had many odd sayings that never made sense to anyone but her. The oddest one was the one she used most often,

"Don't look at me in that tone of voice, it smells a funny colour."

I never worked out what that meant but to this day I still say it to various little relatives to make them giggle.

When I was young I used to love reading Enid Blyton books, I read everything she wrote but my favourites were always the Famous Five. I was obsessed with them and their adventures and I was particularly impressed with George, the tomboy. She was everything I wanted to be, she was allowed to dress and act like a boy and she would go around telling people whatever she thought of them, she wasn't scared of anyone.

The famous five rode around everywhere on their bikes, the weather was always sunny and they always seemed to drag huge picnics with them wherever they went. They always had a big checked tablecloth to spread it all out on and lashings of ginger beer. It was as far removed from my life as you could possibly get, maybe that's why I loved them so much.

In real life my dad worked in a factory that was miles away and every morning at half past six he would leave me and my mother at home and cycle off to the station to catch the train to work. We wouldn't see him again until six o clock at night, this meant that me and my mother would be left alone together all day. We had hours to fill with endless fun.

Most days she would start things off by sending me around to the neighbours with a note asking to borrow money. She was horrendous with money and was always skint. The first few times she had sent me on this errand a few of the more kindly souls had taken pity on me and lent her a few bob. As soon as they realized they were never going to see it again I became as popular as the Black Death down our street. I would get doors slammed in my face left and right and people would run when they saw me coming at them with a note clutched in my sticky little hand.

I often think I have a lot in common with Jehovah Witnesses and when I watch them going door to door in my street being insulted and having doors slammed in their faces I swear I can feel their pain. I still don't answer the door to them though. Although they only have to report back to their god at the end of their shift. I had to face the anti-Christ on my return. I would arrive home empty handed and then run like hell from the fallout.

Of course, I was banned from breathing a word of this to my dad. She was still trying to convince him she was a good housekeeper. When the neighbours stopped being forthcoming she turned to loan men. There would be two or three different ones a week. They would come in, disappear into the front room for a while, then slink out again with their big black books under their arms. I had no concept of loan men and thought they must all be my mother's boyfriends. Why else would I be banned from telling my dad about them as well?

She never would have got away with all this if my Nanna was still next door.

After my Nanna was gone there was no one to see what my mother was up to and report back to my dad so she was free to do as she pleased. She never spent much of her time doing housework. We would spend a lot of our time at her sister's house a few streets away. Her sister was a bit of a good time girl, she dyed her hair jet black and her face was so thick with orange foundation she made todays celebs seem anaemic. My mother said it was called pancake but I'd never had pancakes that thick. I don't know what shade it was but it should have been called day glo.

Apparently, my orange auntie had single handedly kept all the American soldiers entertained when they had been stationed here during the war. It was twenty years later now but she still had plenty of chewing gum and she never ran out of nylons.

Anyway, most days at her house were party days and the house was always full. She had a lot of 'friends', all men, who were always waiting for their ships to sail off again and spoke in funny accents. There would always be drinking and dancing and me and my cousins would be sent outside to play or into the kitchen if it was raining.

I don't recall my mother drinking or dancing but she would flirt with all the sailors when she thought I couldn't see her. Then on the way home she would go on and on about how disgracefully her sister behaved and how she could never be like that. Also, she said if my dad knew what went on at my auntie's he would go mental so we were better off keeping it a secret from him. Something else I had to keep quiet about then, this bloody list was growing longer by the day.

We would usually arrive home about an hour before my dad and in that hour she would quickly peel some spuds and spray some furniture polish around so he would think she'd been slaving away all day. I would try and stay out of the way until bedtime in case I forgot myself and dropped us in it. After I started school it was a bit easier to keep her secrets as I didn't know and didn't want to know what was going on at home.

If I had been a bit older or understood about 'women's problems' I could have maybe kept an eye on the calendar so I wouldn't have been so surprised when the mad woman showed up every few weeks. This woman didn't just keep secrets, she had a temper and she wasn't afraid to use it.

One particular day sticks out in my memory, I wasn't at school this day so either I was too young or it was half term, whatever the reason I was only about five. I was doing something that had made my mother furious (breathing would usually do it) and she decided I needed to learn a lesson, which meant a smacked arse. She started chasing me around the house trying to catch me.

We began our game in the kitchen then the living room and on into the front room, me keeping a few steps in front of her. She was only short so her legs couldn't go very fast, all we needed was the Benny Hill theme tune as we did a few laps of the coffee table and then I headed for the front room door. This was where I made my fatal mistake. Instead of turning right to the front door I made a left and ended up facing the stairs. No time to turn back now so I ran up them two at a time, ending up in the front bedroom.

This was the exact room of my birth where the attempted strangulation had taken place, I was starting to see a pattern here. I could hear her thundering and wheezing just behind me so I made a final lunge for the only place of sanctuary left to me, the huge old double wardrobe in the corner of the room. In the back of my mind somewhere I was thinking if I made it and kept running I just might come out in Narnia. It would be cold in there might be a wicked white witch but it couldn't be worse than this. At least I might get a fur coat and some Turkish delight.

I was stopped short of meeting Aslan and Mr Tumnus by a rough hand clamping the back of my neck, I had been caught. My mother was screaming in my ear, telling me that now she was going to teach me a lesson. I tried to tell her not to bother herself, that's what the teachers at school were for but she was having none of it.

She swung me round with one hand while with the other she tried to land a good hard slap on my backside. I was trying my best to keep my backside out of the way while she huffed and puffed and swung her arm back and forth just missing me every time. We carried on with this dance for a while until we suddenly both had the feeling we were being watched.

We were, the men from the factory opposite were on their lunch break and because it was a nice day they were eating their pack up outside in full view of the bedroom window. They were booing and jeering at my mother like she was the baddy in the Christmas panto. I could hear shouts of

"Leave her alone you bully "and:

"She's only little."

This drove my mother insane with rage. She forgot about my elusive backside for a minute and let go of me so she could fling open the window. Shoving her head out she started screaming at the jeering men to mind their own business or they could have some of the same. More of them joined in with the shouting, it seemed like they were enjoying the banter. This was livening up their lunch break no end. I seized my chance and while she was otherwise engaged I took my backside down the stairs as fast as my legs could carry it and out of the front door.

By the time I got brave enough to come back she'd taken most of her rage out on the men and the fight was gone out of her, at least for now. She wouldn't be beaten though and I knew she'd get her own back when I was least expecting it. For the next few days whenever I had to pull my socks up or fasten my roller skates I made sure my bum was towards the wall.

Of course, this was another thing we weren't allowed to mention to my dad. I don't think he ever really had a clue what my mother was like when he wasn't there. I would be trying to keep everything straight in my head, don't mention where we've been, don't mention who's been here, don't mention the games of chase through the house, don't mention the notes to the neighbours, dear god, the list went on and on. Is there any wonder every night my dad came home to a mute daughter?

His first words every single night when we all sat around the tea table were:

"What have you been doing today then?" followed by:

"Has anyone been?"

I would sit there frozen in my chair like a rabbit caught in the headlights not daring to answer for fear of letting something slip. I would shovel huge amounts of food into my mouth so I could only mime and mumble while all the time feeling my mother's eyes boring twin holes into my forehead. It's a good job her legs were so short; at least she couldn't kick me under the table.

Bloody hell, the Famous Five never had to put up with anything like this.

CHAPTER THREE

Family Fun

I lived for the Weekends when my dad would be home from work, my mother would behave herself then or at least she would calm down a lot. My dad would take me out for bike rides, we would take bags of carrots and other vegetables and feed the animals at the park which was about half a mile from our house. Sometimes he would take me to football on a Saturday afternoon in my bobble hat and scarf. I always felt safe when my dad was around, like I had my very own bodyguard if the madwoman should show up.

He was always doing jobs around the house and always seemed to be painting or decorating. My mother would tell people very proudly that he was ever so handy and I who had nothing to compare with would believe every word. I honestly thought he was good at all that DIY stuff, after all he had built me a spectacular wardrobe for my Sindy dolls. It would be some years before I would come to realise that in fact he was abysmal at all things DIY, but more of that later. For now, he was my hero!

Every week after we had finished our Sunday dinner we would all go for a walk. My parents were very big on walking and I was brought up to think it was perfectly normal to walk for miles without actually having anywhere to go. We would walk on and on until at some point one of my parents would start to feel hungry and we would do an about turn and walk all the way back again.

Sometimes we would walk around the "posh" areas in the neighbourhood to see how the other half lived. These people lived in houses with not only a back garden but a front one as well, all we had was a backyard and a front doorstep right on the street. We would slow down as we passed some of the posher houses and my dad would gaze with envy at their colourful gardens while me and my mother would try and peek through the curtains into their front rooms. God knows what the people inside must have thought, sitting down to their Sunday tea with the three stooges gawking at them through their window.

This walking lark went on for many more years. I dropped out when I got older and realised none of my friends went rambling every week with their mam and dads.

We once went for a week's holiday in Whitby, a seaside place in North Yorkshire that is famous for its hills, practically every street there is built on a steep hill. We took my cousin with us who was four years older than me. She had more normal parents so wasn't used to marathon rambles and so she was in for a shock. She was dragged uphill and down dale morning noon and night for the full week, silently weeping as she limped along on swollen feet. She thought because it was at the seaside we would be spending the week building sandcastles on the beach. Ha, my family didn't spend time on the beach, my parents couldn't see the point, they thought that was boring.

Towards the end of the holiday though they relented and bought us buckets and spades and let us loose on the beach. It was grey and drizzly but never mind, we were finally getting to do something fun. We built a couple of sandcastles and then went for a paddle in the sea. My cousin, bless her, ripped her shoes and socks off her poor blistered feet and plunged straight into the waves, whereupon she promptly stepped on a jellyfish and collapsed in agony. My mother wasted no time in telling her that's why it's more fun to go exploring the town rather than wasting time on the beach. So we set off back to the guest house with my poor cousin limping for a different reason now. At least the pain of the jellyfish sting took her mind off the blisters.

Years later and after years of pain. medication and hospital visits she had to have two artificial knees fitted. She still blames it all on that week in Whitby. We worked it out once that if she had just walked in a straight line from the guest house she could have made it home in two days and been spared another five days of walking.

When we weren't rambling around the neighbourhood we would spend Saturday afternoons in town looking around the shops. Most of the time we never bought anything as we were too hard up, after all my mother was keeping three loan men on the go. We would have to dress up for this as my dad was always big on looking respectable, for forty years he wore a shirt and tie under his boiler suit at work. We would have to polish our shoes and put our best clothes on and my mother would put on lipstick. My hair would be given special treatment which usually consisted of dragging it all off my face and tying the top bit in a ribbon.

The great hairgrip experiment didn't seem to be going anywhere, there were no sign of waves. My hair just seemed to go wherever it felt like on that day, it was quite straight and almost shoulder length in those days. I was living in blissful ignorance, never knowing that soon my mother would pick up a pair of scissors and my life would be over for the next eight years or so.

My dad was really very shy and he would rather die than draw attention to himself, quite the opposite of my mother who didn't seem to care who was looking whenever she had a meltdown. Not that this ever happened when my dad was there, she always saved her performances for the times I (and later my brother) was without a bodyguard.

I'm fast-forwarding a bit here but I remember when my brother was about four and she had taken us both in town without my dad. My brother was getting on her nerves for dawdling or existing or some such thing so she decided to teach him one of her lessons in the middle of a big department store. She grabbed hold of him and went for her trademark move, one hand round the back of the neck, the other cracking the buttocks.

He hadn't yet learned like me how to keep your backside moving so she hit the target every time. He had his own thing though, every time she hit his backside he would make himself go limp on purpose so she would lose her grip on his neck and he would drop to the floor. This would infuriate her so she would pick him up and start all over again. I found this hilarious, it was nice for me to get a reprieve and watch someone else having to play with her for a change.

After a few more smacks and drops to the floor my brother decided to stay down. He wasn't quite as chunky as I had been but he was still pretty heavy to handle when he was playing dead. This drove her mental, she was heaving and pulling at him, trying to get a good enough grip to get him back on his feet but he was equally determined to stay on the floor. This was great, it was better than the wrestling that my nanna used to watch on a Saturday afternoon.

By this time we had gathered quite a crowd, some of the assembled viewers were under the impression that she had knocked my brother out, he certainly was giving a good performance. I started to think maybe they were right until I caught his eye and noticed him smirking, I realised he was doing it on purpose to get sympathy.

After a while my mother sensed that the crowd weren't really on her side. In those days practically everyone smacked their kids, even in public but that was a bit different to actually knocking your four year old son unconscious in the middle of Edwin Davis. In desperation she gave him one final heave, no good, he wasn't going to give in so she did the only thing left to her. She picked up her bags and stomped off, leaving him smirking on the floor and me desperately trying to look sympathetic.

As soon as she was a good distance away I gave him a swift kick to let him know the performance was over for the day and he got to his feet. No one was concerned enough to see if he was ok and now the fun was over they all went back to what they were doing. I was quite tempted to make him take a bow and pass his bobble hat round but we figured we'd better catch her up.

We followed her home, staying a fair distance behind her, I was wondering what we were in for when we got home. If she'd carry on like that in the middle of a big store in front of an audience what would she do when she got us inside behind closed doors?

Luckily for us she bumped into someone she knew on the way and by the time they'd finished gassing it was getting late. My dad would be home soon so it was over for today.

Even though he was only four, my brother had been brought up like me, as soon as he could talk he joined me in the secret service. Before that he could only grunt and point so my mother knew he could be trusted, because of this my dad never got to find out about the days shenanigans. Pity really, he never got to see his son giving his Oscar winning performance.

Best Four-Year Old in the role of an Unconscious Punch-bag.

As I was saying before I went off on a tangent and fast forwarded a few years, my dad was very shy. He would go out of his way to blend in and not attract any attention, his greatest ambition in life was to not stand out from the crowd. God alone knows what he was doing with my mother then. One day a few weeks before Christmas we were all in town, this was when I was still an only child and my mother only had me for entertainment.

On this day my parents were taking me to see Father Christmas in one of the big stores. Unfortunately, it was the same day my dad had just had his new false teeth fitted. He was having a devil of a time just keeping them in his mouth and trying to talk was a nightmare for him. My mother told him to stay in one spot so she could find him again and told him she would take me into the grotto. He mimed back that he was ok with that and off we went, leaving him standing in the toy department. Looking back I suppose we should have left him in the cafe or somewhere, anywhere without lots of shoppers.

He was standing next to a pile of toys looking like a mannequin in his best clothes and new teeth when a woman spotted him and thought he worked there. She proceeded to start quizzing him about the toy she was holding in her hand, she wanted to know if he had any more in the stock room. My poor dad tried his best to answer her without actually opening his mouth but as she couldn't understand him she kept telling him she 'didn't quite catch that'. After the third attempt she managed to catch something though, his teeth as they flew out of his mouth and into her carrier bags. She screamed as if they were really going to bite her and all my poor dad could do was scrabble frantically for his teeth among the woman's shopping.

Me and my mother came out of Santa's grotto just in time to see him running for the doors, new teeth in hand and his face puce with embarrassment. I don't know what it was about my family but whenever we went to a department store there was always something to see.

CHAPTER FOUR

Wee, Custard and Judo

Looking back from a distance, things seem a lot funnier now than they were then and I can sit and laugh about it all now. Mind you, my brother claims he has absolutely no memory of any of it, I think he's just blocked it all out. I hope he never gets hypnotised, it could all come flooding back and send him into a catatonic state with a morbid fear of department stores. Memo to self, keep him away from Paul McKenna or any other stage hypnotists, he's entertained enough crowds in his time.

Quite a chunk of my early years was spent with my cousins, Janice (she of the artificial knees) and Malcom (the other member of my Nanna's fan club). They were my Aunty Dolly's kids, she was my dad's older sister and they all lived just across the playground from us. One of my earliest memories is of a caravan holiday we spent with them at Cleethorpes. I only get odd flashbacks of this as I was only about two but there is photographic evidence of me holding a giant candy floss. At least I think it's me, you can only see two chubby knees and a big bow atop the candy floss. My cousins loved holidays with their parents as there was not a lot of walking involved.

Another early memory concerning Janice is of us both being dragged in to see the doctor who had his surgery two doors down from our house. I was four and Janice was eight and I have no memory of why we were there, I only remember Janice kicking and screaming because the doctor wanted to take off her vest. Eventually she had to be held down and whatever happened next seems to have been so traumatic that to this day neither of us can remember what went on.

The next thing I recall is being in my parents' bedroom the next morning holding a plastic jug in my hand, apparently, the doctor needed a wee sample from me and I was supposed to do it in this jug. In those days no one we knew had an indoor toilet so everybody had a potty under the bed or a bucket in the corner of the bedroom in case they got caught short in the middle of the night. Sounds revolting now but back then it was considered perfectly normal, anyway it was this bucket facing me now. My mother told me to wee in the bucket and try to catch whatever I could in the jug then she departed downstairs leaving me thoroughly confused, not to mention slightly nauseated.

You see, being the typically house-proud woman that she was she had neglected to empty the bucket first and it was still half full of my parents combined urine from the night before. I know, yuck!

Five minutes later I was still there, trying to get my four-year old head around all of this. Why did the doctor want my wee, what was he going to do with it, and what would my mother say when I told her I couldn't manage to do one?

Right on cue she began bellowing up the stairs telling me to get a move on because the doctor was waiting for it. Good god this doctor really seemed to the think my wee was important, trouble was the more I thought about it the more I couldn't go.

What to do?

I was struck by a sudden brainwave so revolting that to this day I still shudder when I remember it and have never been able to share it with a living soul… oh well here goes. Very gingerly, and while holding my nose I dipped the jug into the half full bucket, if this doctor wanted wee so much he could have some of this (I am actually retching as we speak). I wasn't sure how much the old weirdo wanted so I filled the jug almost to the top, then extremely carefully and while trying to avoid looking at it I carried the jug downstairs and presented it to my mother.

She looked slightly shocked when she saw how much I had managed to produce but she didn't seem to notice anything strange. She swiftly decanted some of it into a nearby empty medicine bottle and threw the rest down the sink, never noticing that it wasn't even warm. Meanwhile, I was eying the medicine bottle warily, was this what they dished out when you went to the chemist with a cough?

She disappeared out the front door to deliver the sample to the doctor while I waited with bated breath. Would anyone notice the subterfuge?

When she came back a few minutes later she was acting perfectly normal, maybe I had actually got away with it. For the next few days every time there was a knock on the front door I would be afraid to look up, convinced it would be the doctor on the step clutching the medicine bottle and demanding to know what I had done. But it was never mentioned again, I had committed my first act of fraud and got away with it.

It didn't cross my mind until many years later what a terrible can of worms I could have opened. What if my mother had been pregnant or what if my father had had some terrible disease? What if the doctor had noticed far too many male hormones in the sample and realised that this might explain my sudden desire to be a boy? (he couldn't know about my obsession with the Famous Five and George). I could have found myself on a list for gender reassignment and today I could be a man called Bernard. It's probably a good job the doctors back then weren't very thorough, although I have never trusted one since.

Whenever I got the chance in those days I would escape across the playground to my Aunty Milly's house. She was a lot more careful with her money than my mother and so she always had treats and snacks in the cupboards. Also, she did a mean sponge and custard which she would serve in brightly coloured plastic Tupperware bowls, we couldn't afford Tupperware, that was for posh people.

My mother wasn't so good at baking, in fact her efforts had to be seen (and tasted) to be believed. She thought she was an excellent cook though and would tell everyone she was famous for her pastry, she was - just not for the reasons she thought.

I don't think my cousins were that glad to have me around in those days, I was quite a bit younger than them and must have got on their nerves a bit. I wasn't old enough to play their games, I was too small to fit on their bikes and pogo sticks and I wasn't sophisticated enough to join in with the conversation of Janice and her friends. They would parade around in their mother's high heels and they all carried empty cigarette packets that they had pilfered from their parents. They would fill these packets with rolled up bits of paper and they would sit, pretending to smoke while they gossiped, very sophisticated see.

My cousins also possessed a pair of stilts. I was in awe of these and would watch, green with envy while they tottered up and down the garden path on them. Sometimes, after much sniveling and pleading, they would help me to try and walk on them. They would hold one stilt each to try and hold me up while I desperately wobbled around, trying to manage at least a couple of steps before falling off, it never worked out. They would get fed up and one or both of them would let go and I would go crashing to the ground. I don't think I ever left their house without at least one plaster on my person.

I was a very clumsy child in general and I would fall off, over and into anything that crossed my path, I always fell straight onto my face, bursting my nose and/or splitting my lips open. Whenever this would happen one of my parents would run me to the corner shop and buy me a couple of jelly snakes. For some reason the owner kept them in the fridge so they were always cold and soothing on my poor lips. Come to think of it, maybe he kept them in there just for me as I was such a regular customer. Even today, whenever I stub my toe or trap a finger I always get an urge for a cold jelly snake.

Unfortunately, in later life I would pass this trait on to my daughter. She wasn't clumsy like me but she was incapable of using anything with wheels on without going face first into the pavement. In almost all of her photos up to the age of six she is beaming at the camera and wearing her scabby face like a badge of honour.

While my cousin Janet was busy hobnobbing with her friends and puffing away on their pretend cigarettes her brother Malcom would be teaching me Judo, that was his version of events anyway. He was a bit obsessed with judo at the time, I think he had seen it on the telly or something because I had never heard of it before. He would show me a few moves which usually ended up with me pinned down with his foot across my throat or bent over in extremely uncomfortable positions. After my Aunty Milly heard me screaming for help (which wasn't easy with his sandshoe over my windpipe) she would come running in, hit him round the head with a rolled-up newspaper and take me off to the kitchen for some orange squash and some light mouth to mouth resuscitation.

After that I would have to tread very carefully. Malcom wouldn't be put off that easily when he had found someone to practice on and he would hide in wait for me. I would be passing through the living room on my way to nab a bit more sponge and custard when, without warning he would leap out and take me out with a swift kick to the back of my knees. He was like Kato in the Pink Panther films, lurking behind curtains or hiding in the toy box. One minute you would be going about your business perfectly happily and the next you would find yourself staring at your own bellybutton through the gap in your elbow.

You would think that, with all this going on I would never want to visit their house again but I was there all the time. If I had to be chased around the house by a lunatic intent on showing me what the back of my head looked like I would rather it be in the name of judo.

CHAPTER FIVE

Name That Tune

My mother loved to sing, she was always singing. Not just humming around the house to the radio like most mothers did but full on, from the bottom of your lungs proper loud singing. You could hear her two streets away. She loved to tell the tale of how she had been offered a contract to be a proper singer but had turned down fame and fortune and a life in the spotlight to be a wife and mother. She had given it all up for us she said and we should be bloody grateful.

Strangely, none of our relatives ever remembered this contract. If you listened to my mother's version of events she had been 'discovered' singing in a local club. According to the rest of the family she had only sung once in public and it wasn't in a local club, it was in the little pub on the corner of our street. Apparently in her younger days she had gone in with her sisters for a port and lemon and to listen to the singer that had been booked for the night. The singer got held up and was going to be a bit late so the landlord stood up and asked if anyone could carry a tune and if so would they like to get up and do a few songs while they all waited. This was my mother's big chance, she was out of her seat and grabbing the microphone before the poor man had got to the end of his sentence.

She might have been standing on a stool next to the piano in the tap room of a dingy back street pub but in her mind she was Shirley Bassey, belting out her greatest hits to the adoring audience at the London Palladium, she was in her element. Unfortunately, her time in the spotlight was cut short when the real singer arrived and wanted his microphone back. After a bit of a tussle he took his rightful place on the stool next to the piano and my mother skulked off back to her port and lemon. As far as I could make out, this was the end of her singing career but in my mother's head it was blown out of all proportion. Over the years, she added bits on here and there and actually believed her own delusions. To this day, she still believes if she hadn't turned her back on the spotlights she would probably be a dame by now.

She didn't let this big loss stop her from singing though, oh no quite the contrary. She would let loose at any opportunity, whatever the occasion, it called for a song. Weddings, funerals, birthdays, you name it, she had a song for it. Whenever anyone came in with a birthday cake singing 'Happy Birthday to You' she was straight in there. She would immediately launch into her own version and drown everyone else out with her operatic tones, all she needed were the plaits and a hat with horns on it. I often think that if they'd had the X Factor in her day she would have been first in the queue, harassing the life out of everyone on the panel to get her big break. Thank the Lord it wasn't around back then.

Because of her obsession with exercising her vocal cords me and my dad never sang at all if we could help it, there was no point as we could never match up to her dulcet tones. Also, as I mentioned before, my dad hated to draw attention to himself so in public his singing was confined to miming along with everyone else desperately hoping that nobody had noticed he was there at all.

We had a lot of relatives on my mother's side so when I was young we always seemed to be going to weddings. These were a nightmare for me and my dad, he was too polite to ever get us out of going so we spent many a Saturday afternoon sitting on hard pews in freezing cold churches. We would be ok until the hymn singing started, hymns were my mother's favourite songs after ballads and big band music. She had been forced to attend Catholic school for a bit after her school was bombed during the war so she saw herself as something of an expert.

My dad would be miming away pretending he knew the words (we could never find the right page in the hymn book) while I would be mumbling the bits I knew from school. Meanwhile my mother would be drowning out the rest of the congregation with her high notes, completely oblivious to the relatives nudging each other and sniggering behind our backs. I think they only ever invited us for a good giggle.

One of my earliest musical memories with my mother is from one day before my brother was born. I remember I was sitting on the toilet which was at the bottom of our back yard between the coalhouse and the tin bath hanging on the wall. It was a nice warm day so I was in no rush and for some reason I can't remember I was singing my head off (probably something by Doris Day, I was very much into the film Calamity Jane at the time). I don't know if the acoustics were good in the outside bog or if I was just in a good mood but I was really getting into the song. I finished the final verse, had one more go at the chorus and then wiped my bum and went out into the backyard. To my surprise my mother was standing there by the door, she had been listening the whole time.

"That sounded really nice" she said.

I was dumbstruck, compliments were new to me so I wasn't sure how to respond.

"You sounded a lot better than you do when you sing all those rubbishy pop songs."

Still nothing from me, I was racking my brains trying to come up with a response. Then she went and spoiled it.

"Keep practicing though, some of them notes were off key and your pitch was all over the place."

Well thank you Simon Cowell.

Some years later after my brother was born and we had moved to our new house she would treat the new neighbours to some of her repertoire while getting the tea ready. Unfortunately, our kitchen window at the new house faced right out onto the pavement (more of a front kitchen than a back one). She would be warbling and shrieking while the pots and pans were crashing around and all the cats in the district were heading for the hills. She was under the impression that everyone outside must be asking each other who this wonderful singer could be, surely she should be on the telly?

What she couldn't see was my so called new 'friends', rolling around on the floor under the kitchen window, tears streaming down their faces and laughing until they were in danger of cracking a rib. I was mortified, all I wanted was a normal mother who would go unnoticed among all of the other mothers. Now and again one smart Alec would bite their lip and swallow the laughter down long enough to shout encouragement to her, telling her she was so good they had thought it must be the radio. Her considerable bosom would heave with pride and off she would go again, launching into songs from South Pacific while everyone lay down under the kitchen window again and wet themselves.

I used to feel sorry for my dad, riding home on his bike every night, he must have been able to hear the commotion at least ten minutes before he rode into view. I would have been tempted to just keep pedalling.

To this day, I console myself with the thought that, as bad as it was at least I was grown up and moved out before karaoke was invented.

CHAPTER SIX

Blood Brothers and Holy Water

After my nanna had been banished to her new flat in the back of beyond the house next door to us where she had lived became vacant, not for long though. After a couple of weeks, a new family moved in and I was introduced to my first proper best friend. I was five at the time and we would be inseparable until the time nearly four years later when I would be dragged off in the removal van to our new house miles away.

My new best friend's name was Johnny Simpson and he was a year older than me, also like me he was an only child. His mother doted on him though and the best way she could find to show him how much he was adored was to feed him. She fed him breakfast, dinner and tea and also made sure he had at least three extra meals a day as well as snacks and treats. It's a wonder we ever got time to go off and play because she was forever on the doorstep shouting for him to come in and get something to eat. As you can imagine, he was a big lad.

I don't remember our first meeting but for some reason we got on like a house on fire. I was just getting in to my tomboy stage at this time and we would play army in the old bombed buildings that were still standing from the war. Today it would give the health and safety people a stroke but back then none of the bombed buildings had been pulled down and all us kids played in them all the time. Some of them still had old, broken furniture in them so we would turn them into dens. We used to get told not to go in them but none of us took any notice and our parents got fed up of dragging us out of them so gave up. After all, if Hitler hadn't managed to demolish them with his doodlebugs we were probably safe enough.

Johnny had proper boy's toys, I had a plastic gun and some plastic cowboys and Indians but he had a real Action Man. I always wanted one but my parents thought it was a bit odd for a girl so they kept buying me Sindy dolls instead. I liked Sindy and enjoyed dressing her up and doing her hair but sometimes I wanted a doll that you could throw out the window and force to climb mud hills. I did try to turn one of my old Sindys into an action man once but it didn't go well. I pinched the scissors from the kitchen drawer and gave her a crew cut, then I dressed her in some spare camouflage gear from Johnny's action man and just for added manliness I gave her a beard with a black biro. It didn't really work though, she just looked like Action Man's transvestite friend.

Me and Johnny were both members of the Joe Ninety club, Joe was was a puppet like the Thunderbirds and he was on telly every week. He was a secret agent and me and Johnny both had secret decoders like his that we had sent away for. We could send messages to each other secretly, safe in the knowledge that even if they found them our parents would never be able to decipher them. It never occurred to us that all they had to do was look at our decoders when we were asleep and all would be revealed. They only consisted of a piece of card with a paper wheel that spun round to show the secret letters. Not that our messages were that exciting anyway, mine were nearly always just pleas to borrow Action

Man and Johnny's were usually describing what he had had for his tea.

I went to a normal primary school a couple of streets away but Johnny went to the Catholic school round the corner so we didn't see each other all day during the week. His school was right next door to the Catholic Church and we would dare each other all the time to run in and pinch the holy water from the font. I would creep in, dip my lemonade bottle in and then run like the clappers in case the priest caught me, I was scared to death of him because he wore a dress. The only other man I had ever seen wearing a dress was Danny La Rue on Saturday night telly and that was confusing enough.

Around this time my mother went to work at the local sweet factory and every Thursday night she would bring home a big bag of misshapes. These were the odd shaped chocolates that the workers had made mistakes with and they were allowed to buy them cheap on a payday. By this time my mother had started to get quite a lot bigger so I think a lot of her mistakes went home with her via her mouth.

Because she didn't get home from work until after school had finished she had arranged that I would go to Johnny's house after school to wait until she got home. We always seemed to get in trouble with Johnny's mother for giggling, for some reason she didn't like to hear us laughing. She said it got on her nerves, she would tell us off a couple of times and then if we didn't stop we would be split up. One of us would have to stay inside while the other was sent to stand in the back yard next to the tin bath. I always got the feeling that she didn't like me very much, I think she might have been a bit jealous that her little boy spent so much time with me. But then again, she was living in my Nanna's old house, maybe she was picking up vibes my nanna had left behind. After all, she had been an over protective mother as well.

Either way, nine times out of ten I would be the one sent outside, especially if it was cold or raining. I would stand at the bottom of the yard pulling faces and messing around to make Johnny laugh, his mother would have her back to the window but he could see me clearly. Even from a distance I would see his shoulders shaking and his chins trembling (he had more than me) as he tried to control his laughing.

One day just before teatime we were giggling again and I got sent outside. On this occasion, the tin bath hadn't been hung back on its hook on the wall and was just sitting there in the yard. I knew Mrs Simpson couldn't see me so I decided to put on a show to try and get Johnny to laugh. I caught his eye and made a big show of pretending to get in the bath, I mimed dipping a toe into the imaginary hot water and then looked up. It was working, I could see Johnny's shoulders starting to tremble.

Getting warmed up now I climbed into the bath and pretended to be scrubbing my back, yep he was trying to hide behind a cushion now. Going for full comedy effect I held my nose, closed my eyes and made like I was going under the make-believe water. Popping back up I could see him trying to stuff the cushion in his mouth, ooh I was funny. I gave a thumbs-up, grabbed my nose again and ducked my head back into the bath. I stayed down longer this time for a better effect. When I popped back up again for the last time I opened my eyes and found myself nose to nose with Mrs S. She had been watching for the last few minutes and she wasn't nearly as amused as her son. I was frog-marched back into the house and made to sit on the kitchen chair for a lecture.

She told me that I was a very naughty girl, she said that God was watching everything I did and if I didn't stop acting the fool he would punish me severely. Blimey this was unexpected, I had no idea he was watching me, I didn't even know he knew where I lived. I thought if he was watching maybe he was laughing as well, it was pretty funny after all.

We weren't very big on God in our house, my mother liked some of his music but that was about it. The only times we ever went to church was when one of the many cousins got married or sometimes to the occasional christening. Even then, we only went so my mother could do her Julie Andrews impression. Still, this woman was a Catholic, she had proper crosses on the wall and everything so I figured she must know about these things. I meekly promised her that I would behave in future and told her how sorry I was. I wasn't really frightened of God though, I was more scared that she would tell the man in her church, the one in the dress.

When she had finished her sermon, she gave me another one, this one a bit less holy. She told me any more messing around and she would throw me out onto the street where I could wait for my mother on my own bloody doorstep. Charming.

After that day, I tried to behave around her and before long she began to warm towards me a bit, eventually she started treating me like one of the family. Whenever they went out anywhere together they would let me tag along with them. About a year after they had moved in they bought a big German Shepherd dog so they would take us on long walks across the fields with him. I couldn't get a break from all this bloody walking.

When we weren't at school me and Johnny spent every minute together, we were like Forrest Gump and Jenny, only with Yorkshire accents. We both loved Dr Who and we were equally terrified of the scary Cybermen. We would sit in the long grass next to the playground across the road and make up stories about them to scare each other. Most times we would end up petrified, convinced they were creeping up behind us through the bushes. Then we would run home as fast as we could in a blind panic, Johnny might have been a big lad but he could always keep up with me.

One weekend after watching a Western on telly we decided to become blood brothers (we had seen two red Indians doing it and it looked cool). We weren't allowed knives so we sharpened a wooden lolly-stick against the backyard wall. When we got a sharp enough point on it we stuck it in our thumbs until we were bleeding and then put our thumbs together to mingle our blood. In those days nobody had heard of aids or hepatitis. All done, we went in for tea, we were sporting matching scabs and I had a bit of extra Catholic blood coursing through my heathen veins.

We carried on hanging out together like this every spare minute we had, we were always together. One afternoon during the summer holidays though our beautiful blood brother friendship almost came to an abrupt end when Johnny decided to propose marriage.

Every girl remembers her first proposal they say and I will definitely never forget mine. We were sitting on the curb at the side of the road, sticking wooden lolly-sticks into the hot tar that was bubbling in the sun, I was seven and he was eight. All of a sudden he blurted out the words that will stay with me forever.

"You know when we're older..... if nobody wants to marry me and nobody wants to marry you .... why don't we...."

That's as far as he got, I put an end to his romantic ramblings by delivering him a swift smack in the mouth. What was he thinking?

"Stop being stupid." I told him "We're blood brothers, we've got a pact."

I was horrified, this was awful, it would be like Laurel marrying Hardy or Tom and Jerry running off to Gretna Green, it was all wrong. Luckily, I had brought him to his senses, he agreed with me completely and admitted he was being stupid. It was never mentioned again, we stopped the bleeding and things went back to normal.

In 1969, the year after the proposal I was bundled off in a removal van to our new house and I never saw Johnny again. I still often think of him and hope I didn't ruin him for other women. I would hate to think he spent his life alone, too scared to propose to anyone else for fear of getting smacked in the mouth.

Still at least I will always have something to remember him by, a scar on my forehead in the shape of an exclamation mark. I got it one winter when we were digging in the snow to make a snowman, he got a bit too enthusiastic with his shovel and swinging it over his shoulder he stuck it in my head. He was very sorry and swore it was an accident, probably it was but every time I see it in the mirror I can't help but wonder. Maybe it was payback for that sunny afternoon in 1968 when I crushed his young dreams by smashing my fist into his face.

CHAPTER SEVEN

Is That a Russian Hat?

I had other friends as well as Johnny but more about them later, first I must speak a bit about my appearance which went downhill fast. When I was six years old some clever dick with a clip board and an eye chart turned up at our school. We all lined up to be tested and before you could say 'what bottom line?' I found myself in the opticians up the road picking out glasses. Mrs S was right, God was punishing me for acting the fool.

To be fair my first pair of glasses weren't that bad, they were pale blue and quite understated. I was lucky, most of the other kids at school who wore glasses had the full National Health jobs, little round specs with the optional sticking plaster over the appropriate eye. In comparison, mine were quite posh. I was feeling ok until it came time to leave the shop, inside things had looked quite normal but outside it was terrifying. The right side of my specs didn't seem too bad, everything looked a bit magnified but that was all, however the left lens had been given the full, lazy eye treatment. This gave the effect that everything was sloping and not a gentle slope either, the kerb at the edge of the road seemed to be a three-foot drop.

My mother was trying to get me to cross the road with her but I was clinging on to the nearest lamppost like grim death. There was no way I could climb down there, it was far too steep.

Eventually my mother managed to prise my fingers from the lamppost and we set off for home. It took a while to get there as every step was a nightmare, I would teeter for a while on the edge of what seemed to me like a massive drop then my foot would touch down on the pavement which was really only a few inches from my feet and I would get such a shock I would fall over my feet and go sprawling. I had always been able to fall over fresh air, I really didn't need this. I was hanging on to the back of my mother's coat as if she were my own personal guide dog.

Meanwhile she was trying to shake me off and telling me to stop making such a fuss, couldn't I see people were looking at us? Was she stupid? I was having enough trouble looking at the floor, I daren't look up at the people. And anyway, since when had she worried about people looking at us, she should be used to people looking at us by now.

After a while I figured out that if I closed my left eye I could just about manage to walk in a straight line but my mother didn't like this either, she said I looked like a lunatic and people would think I was winking at them. She really seemed to care about what people thought today, now she knew what I went through every time we went anywhere. Forced to keep both eyes open I managed to make it the rest of the way by shuffling left to right in a crab like movement. My mother then completely gave up on me and insisted on walking twenty paces behind me. Years later I was reminded of that long sideways shuffle home when I played my first game of space invaders.

After a few days of walking around like this and a lot of chortling from the neighbours I managed to get used to my new eyes. Nobody at school called me four eyes or anything as they were all used to seeing specs by then, every other kid in the school wore them. Some had a plaster on the right eye, some on the left, some like me had no plasters and some looked like they were wearing jam jar bottoms but we all seemed to manage alright.

It's a good job we all figured it out really, imagine playtime with fifty per cent of the kids moving across the playground sideways.

I have a photograph from the Christmas of that year, I had been taken to see Father Christmas again and me and Santa are in the grotto. I am looking extremely serious in my new specs and Santa looks like he is wondering why a librarian is trying to get on his knee.

Not long after I got my specs my mother decided I hadn't suffered enough and informed me that I needed a new hairdo to complete my new look. She had never cut anyone's hair in her life before so really I should have seen what was coming. She took out her sewing scissors, stood me in front of the fireplace without a mirror in sight and proceeded to snip away. After a while I started to get a bit alarmed by how much hair was piling up on the floor, also I was beginning to feel a bit of a draught around my ears. Still she carried on. A few minutes later I started to feel light headed, not just because most of my hair was gone but also because I was starting to have a severe panic attack and couldn't breathe properly. I tried to enquire as to whether she was nearly finished, this seemed to startle her,

"Whoops" she said "I was miles away there."
What?

A few more snips, a few more chunks of hair on the ground and she was done. I looked in disbelief at the huge pile of my hair on the floor, I had always wanted a pet cat, maybe now we could build one.

"Go and have a look in the mirror" she said "it looks a lot tidier now."

I hadn't been aware it was untidy, nobody had ever said anything. With a sinking heart I crept into the kitchen to look in the mirror over the sink. At first I thought some weird boy must be looking over my shoulder, I certainly didn't recognise this person. Then it gradually dawned on me, I was the weird boy.

My mother had really done a job on me, it looked as if she had been cutting around an imaginary pudding bowl. All I had left was a small round thing on the top of my head, it looked as if I was wearing a Russian hat two sizes too small. Also, for the first time in my life I had a fringe, well I say fringe..... she had used the top of my glasses as a guide for the fringe but had neglected to see that she had knocked them askew when she was going at the rest of it. As a result my fringe started at eyebrow level at one side and finished about two inches higher at the other. When I pointed this out to her she burst out laughing and started singing 'A life on the ocean waves'.

See, I told you she had a song for every occasion.

I was mortified, how the hell could I go outside looking like this and what would they say at school? Not long after my dad came in from work, he looked at me as if he was about to ask who I was. I think he thought I must be a school friend come for tea (or an escaped mental patient). Gradually it dawned on him that this strange creature was his daughter who this morning had looked like a girl with proper girl's hair and ribbons. He must have thought I'd been in a terrible accident. I could see how horrified he was but bless him he tried to hide it.

My mother was beaming from ear to ear, proud of her hairdressing skills and still brandishing the scissors determined to even up my fringe. My dad took her firmly by the elbow and propelled her into the kitchen where I could hear muffled muttering and the odd swear word. When he came back I could tell he was trying to put a brave face on. I could hear pots and pans crashing in the kitchen and for once there was no singing. He told me to set the table for tea and disappeared behind his newspaper, he must have been wondering how the hell he was going to blend into the background now when he went out with me in tow. By the time tea was ready he seemed to have pulled himself together. He patted me on the (half bald) head, mumbled something about being cooler in summer then we all sat down to eat.

The next morning when I woke up I was relieved to find it had all been a nightmare. Then I got out of bed and passed the dressing table mirror. Oh my god, it was real, what's more I had to go to school and face everyone. Maybe I could change my name and convince them all I was a new boy, probably not a good idea since I would be wearing a school skirt. In the end I had no choice but to just get on with it and wait for my hair to grow back. On the plus side, I would be spared a lot of agony in a morning, my mother usually brushed my hair for me while ripping most if it out by the roots. Now I didn't really need to brush it at all, I could just shake it out of the window and be good to go. That would save me a good ten minutes every morning.

In the end school wasn't as bad as I had been expecting. I got a few comments but nothing too bad, after all most of the school had terrible hair, it was the era of the nit nurse. This nurse would turn up every few weeks at our school and we would all have our heads checked for lice. A lot of the kids had them and would be sent home with horrible smelling stuff in a bottle and a note to take home. As a result a lot of them would turn up with short hair as it was easier to keep clean, because of this I didn't stand out too badly. Also. a lot of my fellow classmates knew about my Famous Five obsession and my desire to be a boy so half of them thought I was just living out my fantasy. The other half thought I had nits.

I almost forgot to mention here one other attractive quality that I possessed. For a few months when I was about seven I developed a nervous habit (and who could blame me) of sticking my tongue out and licking underneath my bottom lip. I would then wipe the wet bit with the back of my sleeve (told you it was attractive). This resulted in a bright red cracked ugly bit under my mouth that looked a bit like a goatee beard. My mother would crack me round the back of the head every time she caught me doing it but I couldn't stop, I was seriously addicted.

Eventually one morning the girl with the red beard caught the teacher's attention and I was hauled off to the nurse's office. She decided I needed to go to the local clinic just up the road. Every now and then some of the more scabby kids in the school would be rounded up and marched off to this clinic to have their various offending bits looked at. Unfortunately, the only treatment they ever dished out there was this horrible bright purple stuff which they would paint onto the scabby area. I have no idea what it was or whether it had any healing properties at all but it looked hideous and stained your skin so much so that no amount of washing could remove it. You would be given a bottle to take home so that your mother could paint you every night and morning. I'm almost sure it did no good at all and was either to let everyone else know that you were unclean or make you feel so humiliated that whatever you were doing to cause the scabs would cease immediately. It was the absolute worst thing that could happen to you at school. If you were purple you were the lowest of the low.

Anyway, this day the nurse decided that she had enough scabby kids on her list to make the trip worthwhile and told me that we would all be going that afternoon. Oh god, this was worse than anything my mother could do to me. Thankfully I went home at lunch time so maybe I could still be spared. I ran home in record time to inform my mother that the nurse wanted me to join the purple people. She was furious, nobody was going to make me look bad (that was her job) and she was going to accompany me back to school and make sure this nurse got the message. We were far too posh to have someone purple in the family, she would never be able to hold her head up in the street.

In the end she didn't come back to school with me but sent a stern note instead informing the school that if I came home painted there would be hell to pay. I suppose that was still giving the nurse the message, literally. Anyway, to cut a long story short none of the teachers or the nurse wanted to tangle with my mother, they had all had some experience with her and me and my scabby chin were given a last minute reprieve. I would be keeping my red beard for the time being.

Not long after these traumatic events my friend's dad noticed my affliction and gave my mother a bottle of glycerine (not nitro) to put on my chin, telling her it would keep the area soft and stop the ugly cracking and redness. He was right, a few weeks later my beard was almost gone and so was my nasty habit. They should have given him a job in the clinic, it would have made a lot of purple people feel a lot better.

Not content with her handiwork up until now, my mother decided she hadn't disfigured me enough and now I needed clothes to go with my new look. She started dressing me in clothes the like of which I had never seen before. I knew she didn't have much money so they couldn't be new ones and besides that I had never seen anything like them in the shops. I was put into trouser suits that had wonderful new colours like mustard and khaki, what's more they came with matching hats. Underneath these suits I would be wearing jumpers that seemed to be knitted from old brillo pads, god knows where she got them all from.

At least I only had to wear these lovely new outfits when I went out with my parents, the rest of the time I could still play out in my jeans with my favourite snake belt. I didn't look like a tomboy anymore though, I looked like a boy called Tom.
I remembered Johnny's mother telling me how God was going to punish me, but what could I possibly have done to deserve this? Surely all this couldn't be

because of my giggling and messing about in the tin bath. I had never used swear words, I had never stolen anything, not so much as a jelly snake unless pilfering the holy water counted. Surely God wouldn't make a little girl suffer this much just for acting the fool. If this is what you got for trying to make your best friend laugh I had better keep my nose clean for the rest of my life.

Little did I know then that this was just the start of a whole new world of fashion and that in a few years my dad would join in trying to find me 'original designs'.

Oh there were some interesting photos to come.

A couple of years ago I was looking through some of these old photos with my little great niece who was about seven at the time. After she had finished wetting herself with hysterical laughter she came up with something interesting. She asked me if my mother made me look ugly so that nobody would want to marry me and I would have to stay at home and do the housework. Hmm, out of the mouths of babes, I never considered that at the time. They're a lot more streetwise nowadays.

CHAPTER EIGHT

Put Those Things Away

Apart from my friendship with my blood brother I also had another good friend. Her name was Denise and she lived about ten doors away from me. We were in the same class at school so we spent most days together and after school she would play out with me and Johnny and a few others. Sometimes her big brother George would play out with us as well but he was quite a bit older so he would go off with his own friends. He was handy to know though because if anyone ever picked on us Denise would threaten to set her big brother on them and they would leave us alone. She wasn't the brightest bulb in the box but I liked her just fine and she was my second-best friend.

She was a bit of a tomboy as well but her parents would never let her wear jeans or trousers, she always had to wear a dress or skirt. This could be a bit embarrassing for her when we were wriggling through the windows of the bombed buildings. Everyone in the street had got an eyeful of her knickers at one time or another but she didn't mind that much. Also, her knees were so scabby she looked like she was permanently wearing red knee pads. I thought her parents were cruel to make her go through all that but she probably thought the same about mine when she looked at my hair.

In all the time we were friends (about four years) I never saw the inside of her house. Her parents wouldn't allow her to take any friends home to play, I think her mother was a tidy freak. Their house was bigger and posher than ours, also they were the only family in the street with a car although none of us ever got to ride in it. Her dad spent more time cleaning it than he did driving it.

Denise was with me one day when we were accidentally given our first lesson in sex education. We were playing out after school one day before tea, everyone else was doing something that day so it was just the two of us. We were roller skating up and down the street, well sort of, we only had one pair of skates between us so we were sharing them. We would take it in turns to wear both of them or we would each put one on and skate up and down in sort of a three-legged fashion. We enjoyed it even if it looked a bit strange.

We were happily hobbling along when we were joined by Margaret Dobbs from round the corner, she was older than us, we were about eight and she was eleven. We weren't supposed to play with her as our parents said she was a rough girl from a bad family and they were all a bit strange but we always talked to her when we saw her. We weren't snobs and everyone was equal in our eyes even if they had dirty necks and nits.

Anyway, this day after we had exchanged the usual pleasantries she lowered her voice, looked up and down the street to make sure nobody was watching and then asked us if we knew were babies came from. I said yes of course I did, the doctor brought them in a black bag wrapped up in cotton wool. Denise looked a bit confused at this and said she thought it had something to do with a stork in a gooseberry bush, I told you she wasn't very bright. Margaret laughed at this and told us they were just stories our mams and dads made up. She told us if we went somewhere secret with her she would tell us the truth. We were intrigued at this so she took us up the back passage (pardon the expression) to explain all.

She explained everything alright, every full gory detail, looking back now she certainly knew a lot for an eleven-year old. The only trouble was we didn't believe a word of it, when you're eight years old the mechanics of sexual intercourse sound physically impossible. We thought she was insane, what she was telling us was too ridiculous for words. Our parents were right about her, she wasn't right in the head.

When she had finished educating us we thanked her for her time and went back to our roller skating, trying not to laugh until she'd disappeared back around the corner. We told each other she was a nutter and said she must be mental to believe all that. We wondered how she'd come up with all that nonsense. After another ten minutes we'd forgotten all about Margaret and her strange ideas and we were getting hungry. It was time for tea so we said our goodbyes and went home.

I never gave any of this another thought until the next day. I had been home from school for a while when there was a knock on the front door, it was Denise's dad and he wanted a word with my mother. I was ushered back inside while he and my mother had a hushed conversation on the doorstep. I was straining to hear what they were saying but couldn't make any of it out. I wondered if my mother had been borrowing money again and if Denise's dad had come round to demand she pay up what she owed. I hoped not, my dad was due home soon and I didn't need any more secrets adding to my list. It was long enough already.

Finally, my mother came back in, flinging the door open she fixed me with one of her looks. Oh God, what had I done now? I quickly racked my brain, trying to think of anything I had done lately that might lead to a game of chase around the coffee table. If that's what she had in mind she'd better hurry up or my dad would come home and catch us playing dodge the slap.

Instead of rolling up her sleeves she demanded to know what filth Margaret Dobbs had been filling my ears with. I was gob smacked, how did she know about that? What I didn't know was that behind my back Denise had gone straight home and repeated everything Margaret had told us to her dad. Every last word apparently, she had found it so funny and unbelievable that she thought her dad would find it hilarious as well. He didn't.

My mother was furious, how could I talk to that girl, I'd been warned enough times and now she was going to have to tell my dad about all this. All what? I was baffled. I tried to tell her that all Margaret had told us was a load of nonsense, why was everyone making such a big fuss? It's not like any of it could be true. Suddenly it began to dawn on me that maybe there was something in it, why else would there be all this commotion? I started to ask my mother if any of it was true, and where did the doctor and the black bag come into it then? And why had someone told Denise all that rubbish about storks and gooseberry bushes? It was about time these grownups got together and sorted their stories out. Before I could get half of this out she told me to listen carefully because she was only going to say this once. Then she fixed me with an evil stare and told me that I must never, never...NEVER, let a boy put his thing near my thing.

What thing, what was she on about now? I tried to ask her, but all she'd say was that I knew exactly what she meant and that was the end of it, we would never mention it again. Well that would be easy, I couldn't mention it because I didn't have the foggiest idea what she was on about.

If she ever told my dad about any of this I never heard about it. My dad would rather have pulled his own eyeballs out through his nostrils than discuss any of this with me.

The next day at school I found Denise and asked her if she knew what was going on. She had no idea (no surprise there) and she was just as bewildered as I was. All she had tried to do was tell her dad a funny story and now he wouldn't look at her and her mother wouldn't stop crying. We had started a right kerfuffle here and we didn't have a clue how we'd done it.

After a few lengthly discussions while we were doing our three-legged roller skating we came to the conclusion that our parents were as mad as Margaret was and obviously, they had all been listening to the same daft stories. We carried on with life as we knew it and didn't discuss it any more. Even so I still made sure that whenever me and Johnny were playing with our toys and guns and stuff we kept all our things separate from each other. Just like my mother told me.

CHAPTER NINE

Orange Knees and Wise Men

After all the trouble Margaret Dobbs had caused, we stayed clear of her from then on. I could annoy my mother enough on my own, I didn't need any assistance. Denise's dad managed to look her in the eye again after a few months and her mother eventually stopped crying and went back to her tidying. Everything was normal again.

We were still playing all our usual games, the weather was nice and warm and Denise's knees were still as scabby as ever. That summer turned out to be an exciting one for us, god knows where it came from but one day a huge lorry rolled down our street dragging an ancient old steam roller. It was unloaded and plonked in the middle of the playground. Whoever it had belonged to had decided that it would make a great attraction for the local kids to play on and so it took pride of place between the swings and the knackered old seesaw. It was a big event and the local paper came out and took a photo of all the kids in the neighbourhood climbing all over it. I don't know where I was that day but I missed my fifteen minutes of fame. A lot of my friends were in the photo which was printed in the paper. My cousin Janice still has the picture among her old photos.

Again, it would be a Health and Safety nightmare nowadays but back then this steamroller was the best thing any of us had ever seen. It was huge and was covered in so much rust that anyone who played on it went home bright orange. from a distance, we all looked really tanned. You could open its hatches and turn the big steering wheel round and round, it was brilliant and we all loved it. It was massive and you could climb right up onto the top of it really high up. As you might expect being the dainty, co-ordinated child that I was I took a good few tumbles off it. One time I fell right off the very top and landed on my back on the floor below. It was concrete, we didn't have grass or bark chippings in those days, we were hard. I remember landing with such a bump that I knocked all the breath out of my body and had to lay there for ages until I could move again. Nobody paid any attention to me while I lay there, no one checked to see if I was ok, if I was bleeding or broken (or dead). They just carried on stepping over (and on) me until I picked myself up. Today's kids would have paramedics and ambulances, police cars and social services getting involved but back then we didn't even tell our parents we had fallen off it. We just wiped off the blood and got back on.

When we went home none of our parents ever noticed our cuts and bruises anyway as we were so orange.

Another bit of excitement that year was going on in Johnny's house, his parents were the first in the street to get a colour telly. It was quite an event and being as I was almost a member of the family I was invited in for the first official viewing. It was amazing, I had never seen anything like it, the green was so green, the red was so red and the Blue Peter garden looked brilliant. I sat transfixed for so long that I had to be asked to leave as they all wanted to go to bed. When I took my leave Johnny's dad was watching Pot Black, the snooker programme. It was so colourful I even wanted to stay and watch that but Mrs S forced me out of the front door. Ten minutes later they noticed my nose pressed up against the window and drew the curtains, the show was over for the night.

When I got back to my house next door my dad was watching Pot Black as well, it wasn't the same though. A few feet from where my dad was sitting the players were potting bright pink, blue, green and yellow balls but on our telly the balls were just several different shades of grey. My dad said it made no difference to him, what you'd never had you didn't miss. I was missing it already and I'd only been home five minutes.

It would be another ten years before we had a colour telly. We had the same black and white set for years, we didn't even own it, it was a rented one. Even though my mother was working as well now we never seemed to have many luxuries. Christmas was always brilliant though, I don't know how they managed it but I always had loads of presents. I would wake up about four in the morning to find a pillowcase full of presents on the end of my bed and usually a couple of big boxes as well. Every year there was always a massive bar of chocolate and a couple of annuals, usually the Beano or Dandy. It was my Christmas tradition to stuff myself sick with the chocolate, read my annuals and then go back to sleep for a bit leaving the rest of my presents to be opened when I woke up again.

One year I had asked for a walking, talking doll and at about four thirty on Christmas morning, while half way through my big bar of chocolate I decided I couldn't wait until later to open it. I was too excited and wanted to have a look at my doll now, I found the biggest box and started ripping off the wrapping paper. When it was all off there was my doll in all her glory, she was the biggest doll I had ever owned. She stood about three feet tall and had a beautiful flowered dress with a little apron and long, thick blonde hair tied in a big ribbon. I was entranced with her.

I had never seen a walking doll in action and stupidly I thought she would actually walk around the room on her own. In my mind, all you had to do was pull this string on her back and off she would go, I didn't know you had to hold its arms and manoeuvre it around. So, standing her up on her feet (she also had white ankle socks and shiny black strappy shoes) I pulled the string, let go and waited for her to start walking. She went face first into the bedside table knocking the bedside lamp over and everything else I had piled up on there. I didn't know that pulling the string would only make her talk, however I soon found that out. Whoever had made these dolls had put in an extremely loud voice box. She let loose with an ear-splitting noise not unlike the sound of my mother singing in the kitchen.

"Please take me for a walk", she shrieked.

Well I was trying to, it wasn't my fault she walked like she'd been at the Christmas sherry. I tried again, standing her back up I pulled the string a second time. Once again, she went crashing to the floor this time screaming,

"Please get me a drink of water."

"Not until you do what you're supposed to you idiot" I hissed under my breath.

I was running out of patience now, I was starting to think there was something wrong with this doll. I was just in the middle of standing her up again when I heard movement on the landing outside my door, I had woken my parents up. Oh well, seeing as they were up.

I gave the string another pull and waited for this bloody doll to do what it said it did on the box. She was just taking yet another nose dive to the floor when my bedroom door flew open and in came my mother, dressing gown askew and hair all over the place. She opened her mouth to start shouting at me but the doll beat her to it.

"Tell me a story" it screeched.

Judging by the look on my mother's face I figured it was going to be out of luck.

"What the bloody hell are you doing" she shouted (my mother, not the doll).

"Its four-o clock in the bloody morning."

"Merry Christmas" I tried, (well it was worth a shot).

"Can't you hear all that racket outside?" she answered, completely ignoring my Season's Greetings.

I suddenly became aware that every dog in the street was howling like crazy. I hadn't been able to hear it for the commotion Suzy Walker (the name on the box) had been making with all her shrieking and vandalism of my furniture. She had driven all the local dogs nuts, that voice must have been of a certain frequency so that every dog in the neighbourhood had been rudely awakened.

Well I was the one in the doghouse now. My beautiful new friend was snatched up from the floor and marched out under my mother's arm.

"You can have this back in the morning" she snapped. "You almost gave your father a heart attack, he thought the little green men had bloody landed."

She switched off the light and stomped off back to bed, a minute later I heard a bump as the doll fell off my parent's bed.

"I've been a good girl" she screeched.

I snuggled back down under the covers, I didn't think my mother would agree with her.

That little episode apart we always had good Christmases. My dad would be off work for at least a week and my mother would be in a good mood. I suppose that could have had something to do with the sherry and the martini we got in every year. She would love it when the kids from the other streets would come around singing Christmas carols. They would hardly get more than a couple of words out before there she was, joining in and completely drowning them out. She lived her life as if she was constantly waiting to be discovered, bursting into song at the most inappropriate moments in the strangest of places. It was as if she thought that at any minute in the corner shop or the doctor's waiting room, the 1960's version of Simon Cowell would stroll by, hear her warbling and sign her up on the spot to be the next big thing. It never happened.

The only black spot on my Christmases after the age of five were the school Christmas plays. The teachers always tried to make sure everyone got a part in them even if they were only on stage for a couple of seconds and their own mothers wouldn't recognise them in the stupid costumes. I lived in fear of my mother showing up and humiliating me at the

Christmas play. It wasn't only her singing that worried me, she would heckle as well. I still cringe at the memory of Joseph making his first appearance on stage and my mother telling him to pull his socks up. It would be bad enough a mother embarrassing her own child on stage, never mind someone else's. God knows how she never got beaten up in the playground.

One year, my acting talents must have impressed Miss Parker because I was given the grand part of second tree from the left. I put my heart and soul into the role and learned how to shake my bits of green crepe paper about in all manner of ways. You can imagine my surprise when twenty minutes before curtain up on opening night, Christopher Caldwell threw up backstage after a dodgy mince pie and I found myself promoted to second wise man.

My leaves and branches were quickly removed and I was bundled into somebody's old dressing gown and had a tea towel slapped onto my head. I had fifteen minutes to learn my lines, actually I only had the one.

"I bring frankincense."

It seemed like no time at all before we were on the stage. I can't remember who Wise Man number one was, but Wise Man number three was my Arch Enemy Maureen Feeny. I have no idea why she was my enemy but I suppose it must have been a big thing back then. Anyway, just after we made our grand entrance I became aware of her whispering at me from behind, something about smells I think. I tried to ignore her and concentrate on my upcoming big line but she began gently nudging me. I wasn't having any of that so I started surreptitiously digging her back with the elbow that was out of sight of the audience.

She starting shoving instead of nudging so I started digging even harder with my elbow. She was bigger and heavier than me so when her shoving got more violent I was having a hard time staying on my feet. It was nearly time for my big moment, Wise Man number one was getting in position ready to present Mary (Susan Harkwright) and her new born doll with the gold. Clutching my frankincense (a coca cola bottle wrapped up in Christmas paper) I prepared to step forward and deliver my line.

Just as I was psyching myself up, Maureen Feeny let loose with an almighty push that sent me sprawling towards the manger, the audience began to titter. How dare she ruin my big moment. I regained my composure, returned to my place and gave her a swift kick to the leg. Some of the audience were sniggering now. We were staring each other down when I became aware of Miss Parker signalling wildly from the wings, it was my turn to take my place beside the manger. I stepped up, delivered my big line and presented my gift. Then I stood aside and waited for Maureen to present her Myrrh (a wrapped-up bean bag). She gave her gift to Mary (Susan) and the baby Jesus and then came and stood beside me and the other wise man, who was completely oblivious to the fact that his two companions were engaging in secret fisticuffs.

At this point there was to be a communal sing song where we all joined in together, even the donkeys and sheep and trees. I had enough to worry about here, dreading that I would hear the familiar warbling that meant my mother had decided we needed her musical expertise and was joining in. I really didn't need to keep fighting as well but Maureen wasn't prepared to give up. She continued with the pushing and shoving, hiding her movements inside the massive dressing gown she was wrapped up in. I tried to move away a few steps but she kept following me and continuing with the sly digs. I tried to fling my arms around as if I was getting carried away with the music, each time making sure my elbow connected with her stomach.

Looking across to the wings, I could see Mrs Hardwitch (the worst teacher in the school) giving us the evil eye. Her face was very red and I'm sure her fists were clenched, I had a sense that we might be in trouble here.

I wasn't wrong, as the song came to an end the curtains started to close. As soon as they were shut we all had to stand in line and be ready to take a bow when they reopened. Mrs Hardwitch took this opportunity to run onto the stage and grab me around the neck with one hand and Maureen with the other. Hissing at us that we would never be allowed in a play again and that we had shown up the full school she started to drag us off the stage. Unfortunately, she had misjudged the time it took for the curtains to be opened again. This meant that the audience were treated to the sight of two wise men being manhandled from the stage by a burly woman wearing a Santa hat. I like to think that's why they applauded for so long, my big moment might have been ruined but at least I was being appreciated.

For once my mother took my side and told me not to worry and that it was all Maureen Feeny's fault. She said it was because her mother was Irish which makes no more sense to me now than it did then. After that we went home to open the Quality Street and it was all forgotten about.

Mrs Hardwitch's threats didn't come to anything either as not long after that she left to work at another school. Despite being told that we would never work in this town again the next Easter saw me and Maureen Feeny on stage once more. This time dressed as blackbirds, wearing paper beaks and sitting in a giant cardboard pie.

CHAPTER TEN

Big Trouble with Little Sally

Not long after the sex education saga a new girl moved into our street, her name was Sally and she was a year younger than me and Denise. She too was an only child and her mother was a single parent which was very unusual in those days. Nobody had divorced parents, your mum and dad stayed together until death, even if they hated each other's guts. All the mothers in the street were very nice to Sally's mother, to her face anyway. Behind her back, they whispered that she was no better than she should be (whatever that meant) and all the dads on the street were banned from doing any jobs for her. Sally started to play out with us straight away and we were allowed to play in her house sometimes. Her mother might have looked like a trollop (I didn't know what one of those was but I'd heard a woman in the corner shop say it) but she had a massive piano in the front room. She used to let me play on it sometimes, I thought I was quite good and would tinkle away for ages until she started to develop a twitch and I would have to go home.

Sally was a quiet girl and looked up to me and Denise because in her eyes we were older and wiser. She would do whatever we asked of her without question and followed us around everywhere like a little puppy. One Sunday afternoon though I almost got her (and me) into the worst trouble of her life.

It started harmlessly enough, Sunday dinner was over and for some reason for once my parents didn't want to go walking that day. The weather was lovely and warm and all the other kids had gone off visiting their grandma's or somewhere else leaving me and Sally the only ones in the street. We decided to walk around the block (I must have been having walking withdrawal) which usually took five or ten minutes as it was only a small block. We told our mums where we were going and set off on our leisurely stroll. Everything was going well until we came to the top of the street, instead of turning right to go back home I was suddenly overcome with a need to go left onto the main shopping road. We were never allowed to go that far on our own but I was feeling reckless. Sally was a bit unsure at first but I convinced her we'd just walk for a couple of minutes and then turn back. Because she thought I was older and wiser she agreed and off we went.

We walked up to the first street and then I convinced her to just walk a bit further up to the next one, there was no one around at all so feeling brave we kept going. This was quite exciting now, we knew we were doing wrong but it felt good to be doing it. We toddled along, me telling her not to breathe a word of this little adventure and her agreeing with me like the sweet little lapdog she was. After a while we suddenly realised that we'd gone a lot further than we had intended, I had never been this far from home without my parents. We had lost track of time and had no idea how long we'd actually been gone. Sally started to panic that her mother would be looking for her, I was actually having palpitations myself but I told her if we ran back really fast they probably wouldn't have missed us yet. Holding hands, we legged it as fast as we could back towards home, Sally was quite a bit smaller than me so I had to half drag her behind me.

When we reached the corner of our street we slowed down to catch our breath, trying to compose ourselves and look innocent. When we thought we'd managed this we turned the corner into our street.

Straight away we saw Sally's mother, my parents and half a dozen other adults from the street all milling around. Oh no, we hadn't got away with it and from the looks of it they were forming a search party. My mother saw us and pointed and they all came running up the street towards us. Without knowing what I was going to say I whispered to Sally to keep quiet and go along with whatever I said. Looking at her she seemed too frightened to speak anyway but she nodded at me.

The posse all reached us at the same time, they were all screaming at once wanting to know where the hell we'd been, what the hell we thought we were playing at and did we have any idea how worried they'd been, Sally's mother was crying. Then they all looked at me. I was the oldest, I was in charge, how could I be so irresponsible, on and on they went. My mind was going ten to the dozen, trying to think how I could possibly get us (or rather me) out of this. Suddenly I was struck by the stupidest idea ever.

"It was a big lad." I blurted out "He made us walk up the road with him and he wouldn't let us come back."

They all exploded at once.
"What lad?"
"Who was he?"
"What did he look like?"
I was still trying to think on my feet.

"I've never seen him before, he had black hair and a leather jacket."

Oh my god where had that come from? The only lad I had ever seen wearing a leather jacket was on West Side Story, the film that me and my mother had watched on telly the week before. I was describing one of the all singing, all dancing gang members. On hearing this they all went completely mental.

"Why didn't you run away?"

I sneaked a look at Sally whose eyes were now nearly as wide as her mouth. Then from somewhere I suddenly came out with the worst lie I ever told. To this day, I am ashamed to admit it even to myself and unless in later life Sally came clean, me and her are the only people who know about it.

"He had a knife." I blurted.

As soon as the words left my mouth I instantly regretted them, I thought I heard a small squeak from poor Sally who was standing next to me quaking. Well as you can imagine when they heard this they all completely lost it and who could blame them. In my stupid head, I was picturing a butter knife or something, we played with butter knives all the time. When we were bored, we would pinch one from the kitchen and chisel out the mortar from between the bricks of the passage. The parents were picturing something quite different. In their minds, they were seeing Jack the Ripper chasing two little girls up the road on a for a spot of Sunday afternoon disembowelling.

At once we were both being hugged by the crying women while all the men went running off to hunt down this non-existent leather clad fiend. Sally was looking at me in complete horror, I could see the shock in her eyes at discovering her nice new friend was in fact a lying psychopath. Oh, my god, what the hell had I done? If I got caught lying about this, it would be a million times worse than if I'd just owned up to wandering off. As I was taken off home I caught a last glimpse of poor Sally being led off by her mother, she was white as a sheet but still not talking (I don't think she was capable of speech by this time) I was praying she wouldn't crack.

Half an hour later the men were back, having failed to find anyone matching the description I'd given (not surprising really). Another hour after that we were having our tea just like any normal Sunday and that was that, it was all over. It was as if none of it had happened at all and it wasn't mentioned again, everyone just carried on as normal. I couldn't believe it, I'd got away with it although my knees were still knocking for days afterwards. I know it's not a fitting punishment but I felt guilty for ages (still do) and I lived in fear of being found out for weeks.

Poor Sally, she kept my awful secret and never blabbed but she stopped looking up to me and it wasn't so easy to tell her what to do any more. So, one good thing came out of the awfulness, it made Sally more assertive.

Can you imagine that happening nowadays? There would be police everywhere, the street would be swarming with reporters, counsellors would be brought in. I would have to do an e-fit of the man from West Side Story, and me and poor Sally would be filmed walking up and down the road in a reconstruction for Crimewatch.

Looking back I really should have owned up. In my defence though things just got away from me, once I started lying I couldn't stop and the lie just got bigger and bigger. If it's any consolation I never told a lie that bad ever again and even now I break out in a cold sweat and shake uncontrollably whenever I hear a song from West Side Story.

CHAPTER ELEVEN

Engine Oil and Diamantes

One evening when I was almost nine my dad came home from work, had his tea and then asked me if I wanted to go to work with him. I said I'd love to I'd had enough of school already. No such luck though, he told me he'd got a job for an hour or two after work as the night watchman at the engineering factory opposite our house. He said if I behaved and didn't tell anyone (oh my god I was keeping my dad's secrets as well now) I could go with him. So, at about seven o clock off we went, we waved goodbye to my mother and left her in the kitchen giving her usual after tea concert.

I enjoyed myself so much that first time that from then on, every time my dad went to do his rounds I went with him. To get into the building we had to climb through a little door that was built into the big main doors. My dad had his torch because it was dark everywhere and dead spooky, the smell of engine oil was everywhere. To this day, I cannot smell engine oil without being reminded of that factory all those years ago. This was another example of something you would never get away with today, there must be so many laws, rules and regulations about taking a child into somewhere like that.

Come to think of it my dad really shouldn't have wanted to take his precious little princess (even one with a pudding bowl haircut) into such a dangerous environment. Never mind the safety aspects, what if we had come across someone robbing the place, what would have happened then? I told you my dad was shy, maybe I was there in case he had to confront someone and didn't like to ask what they were up to himself.

I used to imagine that there were robbers around every corner, I don't know what we would have done if we had ever encountered any I would have to think back to the last Famous Five book I had read and ask myself what George would do. Probably tell the robber he looked like a dirty gypsy, hit him over the head with a bottle of ginger beer and tie him up with Timmy's dog lead until the constable arrived. Then he would be thrown in jail for the rest of his life with nothing but bread and water and given a jolly good thrashing every day. I was starting to have my doubts about George. I didn't hear the word "lesbian" until I was older but once I did everything about George started to make sense.

No matter how careful I was I always managed to come back from the factory every night covered in muck. My mother got so fed up with having to get oil out of my clothes she asked my dad if he could get me a boiler suit like his. I wouldn't have minded this at all, it would have looked better than most of my clothes.

Around this time, I had to go and get my eyes tested again, I was hoping they would have got better by now and I wouldn't need my glasses anymore, no such luck. The optician decided I needed new lenses and so I was invited to pick some new frames as well. My mother took this as a sign to gate crash my invitation and she descended on the rack of frames on offer. I wanted something discreet that wouldn't stand out, I had enough going on already to attract attention. My mother didn't agree though, she found what she called the perfect pair hidden at the bottom of the rest. All I can say is I wish they'd remained hidden. They were bright red which on its own was bad enough and they extended at each side into huge wings. At the edge of each wing was a huge glittering diamante, they were the ugliest things I had ever seen. I was horrified and begged and pleaded with my mother to put them back where she'd found them. She insisted I try them on and when I did they looked even uglier if that was possible.

They were huge, I felt like I would never make it through the door they stuck out that much. I kept getting an image of those big red cows, the ones with the massive horns. Even the woman who was serving us looked horrified, I don't think she believed any mother could make her child wear something so horrific. She looked really uncomfortable and kept avoiding my eyes while she served us, not easy in those things.

Back then nobody had heard of Dame Edna Everage, I don't think she'd even been invented. I still believe that somehow, somewhere Barry Humphries once saw a photograph of me in my specs and Edna was born.

All my pleading for different glasses fell on deaf ears and I left the shop wearing the big red monstrosities, I have never felt so conspicuous in my life. If we'd had an international space station at that time the astronauts would have been looking out of the window saying

"Bloody hell, look at the sun glinting off those diamantes."

Because they'd fiddled around with the lenses once again I had to walk home like a lunatic teetering on the edge of every kerb edge and walking on a slant. At least last time I only looked like a lunatic because of the way I was walking, this time I looked like an Aberdeen Angus staggering around. Scratch that, this time I looked like an Aberdeen Angus with a pudding basin haircut and a fetching trouser suit.

I couldn't understand how my mother could do this to me. I always thought a mother wanted a daughter so she could dress her up to look pretty, not pretty hideous. To cap it all off she kept telling me they were just like my Aunty Dolly's glasses and how we could be twins. Now I loved my Aunty Dolly, she was a lovely woman but she was no oil painting and she was thirty years older than me. What would my dad think to this latest development?

Not a lot as it turned out. When he came home that night I was waiting at the front door absolutely certain that when he saw what had been done to me he would put his foot down and tell my mother to take the bloody awful specs back to the shop. He came in, peered at the little old lady scowling up at him then he patted me on the head and said,

"Hmm, they look nice, you remind me of your Aunty Dolly."

What? What was going on here, why wasn't he defending me? I came to the conclusion my mother must have infected him. Either that or he was thinking of his own safety when he did his rounds at the factory. If any robbers happened to be hanging around one look at me peering through the darkness at them and they'd be gone.

I was a guard dog.

The next day at school my new look was a big hit. Everyone spent the day laughing and pointing (especially the teachers) and by the time half past three came around I had at least fifteen new nicknames. At least nobody could get too close, with the size of the wings on my new glasses anyone who came within a foot of me was in danger of being speared. That's if they weren't already blinded by the megawatts of light reflecting off the sodding diamantes.

How much could one person be expected to take.

CHAPTER TWELVE

Apple Pie and Batman Ears

My mother did a lot of singing in the kitchen but not much else. Most nights she hurriedly slapped something together just before my dad got in and that was that. Once a week though she would come over all domesticated and on would go the pinny, it was baking day. She would be in there yodelling for hours flinging flour around and rattling bun tins, the air would fill with the wonderful aroma of baking and it would make your mouth water. Sadly, this only lasted until everything came out of the oven, nothing ever came out right. You could taste the disappointment in the air, mind you even that tasted better than my baking.

I don't know if you've ever seen pastry come out of the oven whiter than when it went in, I think it was something only my mother could achieve. It was quite amazing really, like some sort of conjuring trick. Also, if you picked a piece of the pastry up and squashed it between your fingers it wouldn't crumble like it was supposed to, instead it reverted back to dough. It was baking in reverse. I thought for a while maybe there was something wrong with the oven, after all it was the same one that the previous tenant had gassed himself with. I was proved wrong on that though, over the years my mother went through many ovens and the pastry remained the same. In fact, it remained the same for sixty years.

Amazingly she really believed she was good at baking. All my life I have had to listen to her telling all and sundry how she had always been famous for her pastry. She just didn't get it when people would nod politely and quickly change the subject. The worst thing was that she would bake for other people and be convinced she was doing them a big favour. I can't imagine how many of her creations went straight in the dustbin and boy would that dustbin have been heavy.

Years later after I was married with a daughter of my own she was still at it. We would visit on a Sunday afternoon and she would send us home with one of her famous apple pies. We would exchange looks of horror but struggle home with it anyway. I would open the front door, shout to let my husband know that an apple pie was incoming and he would run to open the back door straight away. I would then march straight through to the garden and dump the whole lot out on the grass for the birds. Most of them would have a quick peck and leave well alone, they had been there, done that and still had the stomach ache to prove it. Some of the dimmer ones would give it a go, only to be found a few hours later frantically flapping their wings and trying to get off the ground.

I couldn't understand how everyone else's mothers could bake the same things and always end up with pies that were golden brown and crispy and tasted nice. It wasn't until I got a bit older and started to do cookery at school that I began to realise what was going wrong. One of the first things we ever made at school was an apple pie. We were all given the recipe to follow on the blackboard and apart from a few burnt crusts here and there they all turned out pretty much the same. They looked like they were supposed to and they tasted nice. We knew this because one of the larger girls couldn't wait until she got home and proceeded to demolish hers in the cloakroom letting us all have a sample.

I arrived home with mine and proudly presented it to my mother. She said it looked very nice, maybe a bit well done but we would all have a bit after tea. So, after my dad was home and we had finished our tea I proudly served us all up a piece. It was really nice, my dad was well impressed and my mother finished all hers. I waited for the verdict, would she realise that for all these years she might have been doing something wrong? No such luck, she said it was very nice but my pastry wasn't quite right, it wasn't as moist as hers. Moist, is that what she thought her pastry was? I would rather have called it raw and uncooked.

She asked to see my recipe which I had copied down from the blackboard into my first little recipe book. She looked at it for a few minutes and then said she could see where I was going wrong, my pastry ingredients weren't right at all. She told me all you needed to make tasty pastry was flour, water and large amounts of lard. Oh good god, all these years she had been making everyone lard pies.

I slept on this new information for a while and then decided to quiz her on her culinary skills, I asked her where had she learnt to cook. She told me she had learned everything from her mother, she was the one that had taught her the proper way to make pastry. I did a bit more thinking and then realised that she had learned everything just after the Second World War when everything was still rationed. My grandmother wasn't making pastry like that out of choice, she was doing it because there was nothing to put in with the flour except lard, it was a wartime recipe. Things started to make a bit more sense suddenly, the Yorkshire puddings with no eggs in them, the cakes that would never rise. We were eating as if the country was still on rations.

I never got to meet my grandmother, she died six months before I was born. I wish I had got to meet her though, I have a feeling she could have explained a lot.

As well as the cooking and baking my mother did quite a lot of knitting in those days and I was forced to wear a lot of her experiments, especially hats. She would knit these bonnets that had two pointed ears on them, she said they were quite fashionable but I never believed her. I think she must have been pretty crap at following the pattern as well because the ears on my bonnet always looked a lot bigger than the ones on the front of the pattern book. The little girl in the picture looked very cute in her bonnet which had two discreet little points at each side, mine looked like I was auditioning for the part of Batman. Still at least they hid my haircut.

She also knitted me lots of cardigans both buttoned and zip up. I think she must have been easily distracted when she was knitting as the two sides never really looked like they matched up. One side was always bigger than the other, one arm always much longer than the other so I looked like I had a disability or sometimes a hunchback. Once she was knitting me a cardigan in light blue when half way through she ran out of wool. Not to be put off she dug around until she found some navy-blue wool and carried on. I ended up with a cardigan that was light blue on the bottom half and dark blue on the top.

My mother was dead pleased with the end result, she had invented a new fashion. In fact, she was so pleased with herself she went and knitted me another one, this one was half orange and half lemon. For a finishing touch, she added alternate orange and lemon buttons, I looked like a packet of opal fruits. After that I lived in fear of what was to come next, just the sound of her needles clicking together was enough to make me break out into a cold sweat.

Fortunately for us all my mother gave up knitting a long time ago, not soon enough though that my brother was spared having to wear her creations. No matter how much practice she got she never really improved, also she never learnt to calculate how much wool she would need. As a result, she always ran out and so she would finish off with whatever odds and ends she could find in her knitting bag. It didn't matter if the wool was a completely different colour. Even now I can still remember the sight of my six-year-old brother setting off for school wearing his brand new yellow jumper with the half pink sleeves.

CHAPTER THIRTEEN

Please Don't Do It Yourself

As I mentioned a bit earlier my dad was always going around the house demonstrating his DIY skills. He was always painting and wallpapering and as far as I knew with my limited knowledge of interior design he was good at it. Remember this was the late sixties, the age of psychedelic wallpaper so any mistakes he made were easily hidden among the swirling colours. We were still living in our little terraced house at that time and he couldn't really do a lot with it except wallpaper and paint. Today that house would be deemed unsafe to live in as one of the bedrooms was a complete death trap. We had three bedrooms, my single, my parents double and another small back bedroom over the kitchen.

In the corner of this room was a massive hole in the floor, about three feet across. If you peered down into it, you could see right down into the pantry at the back of the kitchen. Nobody seemed to think this was at all odd and I was allowed to use this room as a playroom as long as I arranged my mother's wooden clothes horse around the hole to stop me from falling in and making an unannounced entrance in the pantry. Until recently I had always assumed the hole was caused by bomb damage during the war, a lot of the streets around us had been bombed. It was only through a chance conversation with my mother all these years later that I discovered the hole was actually caused by my dad removing one of the downstairs chimneys with no idea what he was doing. I was completely shocked to find this out as the house didn't belong to my parents it was rented, I couldn't figure out how he had managed to get away with it without being evicted. My mother told me that they never bothered to tell the landlord and as nobody ever checked up on their tenants back then he never found out. I couldn't believe they had lived in the house for all those years with that guilty secret hanging over their heads (as well as most of the back-bedroom floor).

Anyway, aside from demolishing the place my dad did what he could to keep it nice. He did a lot of stuff with something called fablon in those days, this was plastic on a roll in different patterns and colours. You would walk into our house and at first glance it would look like we had lovely wooden shelves and tables. On closer inspection, it quickly became clear that everything was covered in sticky back plastic, my dad would have been right at home on Blue Peter.

After my brother was born we moved to our first council house, it was almost brand new and had a back garden, a bathroom and not one but two inside toilets. More importantly we had three bedrooms with no sign of any holes in any of the floors. We all felt as though we'd been given a palace. Now my dad had a blank canvas to work with he could really go to town and let rip with his decorating skills. First of all, though he set about tackling the garden, it wasn't very big but it was a dream come true for him. Because we had never had a garden before he had no gardening tools at all but he didn't let that stop him. When he saw how long the grass was he raided my mother's sewing basket for her big scissors and spent a full day cutting the grass with them. He had blisters for weeks.

After he had finished tidying up the garden he turned his attention to the house. The upstairs landing was only small with five doors, three bedrooms, a bathroom and a big airing cupboard. Now most people would paint these doors white wouldn't they, I mean most normal people. My dad however decided what we really needed were rainbow doors, so he painted each one a different colour, we had a green one, a blue one, a pink one, a yellow one and a lilac one. In the kitchen, he thought he would make a real statement, it was the first time we had a real kitchen with fitted cupboards and everything matching, but to my dad it was boring.

To liven it up he bought lots of orange paint and lots of yellow paint and then he proceeded to paint alternate doors, a yellow one, an orange one, a yellow one, an orange one etc. etc. Then he repeated this on all the drawer fronts, alternating orange and yellow until the kitchen looked like an orange and yellow chess board, it was astounding. If I ever wandered into the kitchen wearing my half yellow, half orange cardigan I disappeared. The family could have hours of fun trying to spot me, it was like a 1960's version of Where's Waldo. He carried on right through the place putting his own personal stamp on everything until the house looked like there had been an explosion in a paint factory. It wasn't just an assault on the senses, it was GBH.

I was nine by this time and I was starting to get an inkling that this wasn't completely normal, when I got a bit older and started going to friends' houses I was convinced. All the houses on our new estate were identical on the outside but nobody else's looked anything like ours on the inside. Their rooms had nicely coloured wallpaper, they had normal kitchens and white doors. Whenever any of my friends came to my house I could see the horror in their eyes and I knew they couldn't wait to get home and tell their mothers about ours. I think my dad had invented a new motto for himself,

'Why Settle for One Colour in a Room When You Could Have Twenty-three?'

His main motto though was - 'Nobody Will Notice.'

He applied this motto to all his DIY, holes in walls that needed a bit of plaster were instead covered in hardboard that was nailed on and then papered over, Nobody Will Notice.

Need new tiles? Why bother taking the old ones off first when you could just tile over them with the new ones, Nobody Will Notice.

He had the same problem with wallpapering that my mother had with knitting, just as she always ran out of wool he always ran out of wallpaper. Instead of waiting and going back to the shop for another roll he would rummage around in the shed until he found a half roll that he had used somewhere else, as long as it was roughly the same colour it would do. Then he would finish off the job by applying it to the bit of wall he had run out on. It was never even the same pattern, always a completely different shade, but no matter, Nobody Will Notice.

The fact that your eyes were drawn straight to it the moment you entered the room was lost on him. In his mind, he was so successful at this that he started applying it to carpets too. He would buy a remnant from the carpet shop that was always a bit short somewhere and then stick a piece in from a completely different carpet. He would say it didn't matter because it was in the corner of the room, Nobody Will Notice.

While all this was going on my mother would be standing behind him applauding and telling him how fabulous it looked. I wanted to tell her to stop encouraging him and just tell the truth but then it dawned on me that she really meant it, they were as deluded as each other. This continued for the rest of my dad's days, he never really got the hang of it. A few years before he died I wallpapered my hallway in a fleur de lys pattern and my dad really liked it. He bought the same paper in a different colour and decorated his living room with it. When I went round to have a look I couldn't believe it, he had put the whole lot on upside down. I didn't have the heart to tell him so I just told him it looked nice.

After that whenever he came to my house he would spend ages hanging his coat up in the hallway. I would peep round the doorway and there he would be, staring at my wallpaper with a confused look on his face. I never knew if he was thinking what a big mistake he had made or if he was thinking he was being kind by not telling me mine was on upside down.

The only time I ever remember my parents sticking to one colour in a room was one year when they redid the living room. My mother had a fancy for purple that year and boy was it purple by the time they had finished with it. They started with the purple wallpaper and for once my dad bought enough rolls. This time the doors were almost covered in the same wallpaper as well, he just left a bit of paint round the edges, the paint was a fetching shade of lilac. When it came to accessorising they went completely overboard. They chose a purple carpet, big furry purple rug, purple cushions, purple curtains, if it was in there it was purple. I don't think they had ever heard the phrase 'Less is More'. It was absolutely hideous, if you spent five minutes in there you would come out with the migraine from hell. The only way you could stay in it for long is if you wore sunglasses or kept your eyes closed. My mother loved it though, she thought it was dead classy and glamorous, once again the thought that I was adopted started to resurface.

I was watching telly at home the other day when 'Sixty Minute Makeover' came on, it started me thinking about my dad. He would have been great on that show, he could ruin a house in sixty minutes no problem.

CHAPTER FOURTEEN

The Snitch and the Bee Sting

Growing up I don't remember my mother having any proper friends, plenty of enemies but no friends, she just couldn't get on with anyone. She would be ok at first with new people but after a while she would be unable to keep her opinions to herself. She would end up insulting them in one way or another and they would be out the door without so much as a backwards glance. Either that or she would offer them a piece of pie and they would be out the door much faster.

She didn't get on that well with my Aunty Dolly either although you wouldn't realise this at first when you saw them together. In front of other people, they were polite and friendly to each other but that was all front. In fact, my mother was jealous to death of my Aunty Dolly, because she was another female taking my dad's attention away from her. She was the same way with all females including me and the dog (she was still around and still sniffing me on a regular basis). My Aunty Dolly had no time for my mother either, she thought my dad could have done a lot better for himself. Also, she had been on the receiving end of many a begging note whenever my mother needed money and had never seen any of the cash she lent her again.

My Aunty Dolly was in the Secret Service with me although she didn't know half the secrets I did. She was keeping things from my dad to protect him though, not to keep my mother out of trouble. When I got older she would sit for hours telling me all the horror stories she had gathered over the years about my mother. I think she enjoyed this a tad too much than was healthy.

She was a really heavy smoker my Aunty Dolly. My mother had never smoked and couldn't stand the smell of anyone smoking near her although she would make far more of a fuss than was necessary. If anyone lit up, she would immediately start coughing, waving her hands in front of her face and flinging open the windows. My Aunty Dolly was wise to all this and over the years developed many ways to make sure whenever she had a fag the smoke always went straight up my mother's nose.

For all his shyness, my dad had a few friends from work, one of them he had known for years and sometimes we went to his house to visit. Most of the time we would just turn up unannounced without waiting to be invited, my parents didn't get social niceties. Usually we would arrive at mealtimes and watch his poor wife having kittens trying to stretch the meal to include us. Even I was uncomfortable when they did this and I was really young.

One such night we gate crashed their house in the middle of a party they were giving. My mother made a speech about how fortunate that we'd turned up on that particular night. She didn't get that if we were wanted there we would have been invited. Anyway, this night they had asked all the children of their friends to come in fancy dress (the ones that were actually invited). I stuck out like a sore thumb so the nice lady took pity on me and whisked me off upstairs to find something they could put me in. Ten minutes later I came down the stairs wrapped in bath towels with another large towel on my head turban style. Pinned to the top of my turban was a bunch of real grapes, apparently, I was Carmen Miranda. I had never heard of this person but everyone at the party seemed to find it hilarious, including my parents. I spent the night glaring at them from behind my grapes (they kept slipping) and wondering how they could be so insensitive.

A few weeks later my mother called me into the front room. She was watching an old black and white film on the TV (although everything on our telly was black and white) and she pointed to a woman dancing around.

"That's Carmen Miranda." she laughed "That's who you were supposed to be."

I didn't really see the resemblance; this lady was wearing a beautiful dress and a big fancy head dress. Admittedly she had a bit of fruit going on up there but there wasn't a bath towel in sight, once again I had been made to look a fool in public.

One friend of my mother's lasted quite a bit longer than any of the others, her name was Miriam and she moved in backway to us. I thought she was very glamorous, she had long hair and wore mini dresses the same as Sandy Shaw wore on Top of the Pops. Also, she was from down south so spoke very differently to us Yorkshire folk. She had two little boys, one my age (I was about five at the time) and the other about two years old. We used to go to her house so us kids could play together and she would come to ours. After a while my dad got friendly with her husband and both couples would go out together. Sometimes if Miriam and her husband Jim wanted a night out my mother would babysit for them and she would do the same for my parents when they went out.

I thought she was great and looked forward to the times she babysat me, she would play with my toys with me and read me stories and I used to think what a nice mother she would make. One night I was proved wrong, she let me down very badly and I never trusted her or looked up to her again. I had gone to bed that night not feeling very well and with a stomach ache, Miriam had read me a story and I fallen asleep. I woke up suddenly in the dark and realised it must be quite late, I wasn't sure what had woken me up but I knew something was wrong. Then I realised that my pyjamas felt a lot lumpier than they had when I had got into bed. Oh no, the worst possible thing had happened, I had pooed myself. I was mortified but I didn't dare get out of bed in case it went everywhere. In distress, I shouted for Miriam, she would look after me and I knew she wouldn't be annoyed at me like my mother would.

She came in and realised straight away what had happened, the aroma probably gave the game away. She was really nice about it, she told me not to worry and that accidents happen, it was nothing to be embarrassed about. Then she helped me get cleaned up and into fresh pyjamas before she put me back to bed (it was still clean, I had contained everything in the seat of my pyjamas, I wasn't an animal). She was just heading for the door, evidence in hand when we heard voices and laughing in the hallway downstairs, my parents were back and they had brought people back with them. I begged Miriam not to say anything about my accident until everyone had gone, and she promised me she wouldn't. Then she said goodnight and went out leaving me thinking what a lovely woman she was.

I was just snuggling back down in my bed, Miriam must have only been about three or four steps down the stairs when I heard her screech,

"Here I am, I've just been cleaning up, someone had a bit of an accident Ha Ha."

I couldn't believe my ears, I was mortified, how dare she humiliate me like this? I could hear laughter and someone shouting:

"Phew."

I could have died of embarrassment. I lay there in the dark with my cheeks burning (both sets) and vowed that was it, me and Miriam were over.

Over the next few days I tried to keep my distance from Miriam, if she came in I would leave the room and go play in my bedroom or the back yard. She was perfectly lovely to me, as if nothing had happened but I knew it was all a front and she wasn't the nice person she pretended to be. She had betrayed me.

One Sunday morning a couple of weeks later Miriam popped across to our house. She said it was going to be a really hot day and asked if we wanted to go to the seaside with them in their car (yep we knew two people with cars now). My parents said yes that would be great and my mother started making sandwiches. It was a bit strange that my parents were willing to sit on a beach all day but I was excited, I could put my differences with Miriam to one side for the day and have some fun.

Somehow, we all managed to squash ourselves into the car and set off. In those days, there were no seat belts and you tried to fit as many people into a car as you could manage. You often saw cars going by on a weekend with little faces mashed up against the rear window or little legs poking through the windows, nobody cared. Anyway, after about an hour of being folded up in the back we arrived at the beach, we untangled ourselves, worked out the cramps and we were off.

It was great at first, the grown-ups sat talking under a big umbrella thingy while me and the two boys paddled, built endless sandcastles and played ball. After a couple of hours, we were told to come and get something to eat, Miriam and my mother were setting out a picnic. I was just sitting down to enjoy my meat paste sandwich when it happened. Out of the blue a sharp pain hit me in the shoulder, it felt like someone sticking a red-hot needle into me (not that I had any experience of red hot needles, my mother liked slapping backsides and the odd clip round the back of the head, but she hadn't progressed to torture).

I let out a scream of pain, forgetting all about my sandwich and looked down just in time to see an enormous bee leaving my shoulder, for the first time in my life I had been stung. The pain was so terrible I didn't know what to do with myself. I could hear my mother and Miriam shouting while my mother rummaged around in her bag to find anything that might help. Before she got a chance to do anything Miriam's husband Jim descended on me, shouting that he would handle this.

The next thing I knew he had clamped his mouth onto my shoulder and started to suck on it like he was dying of thirst and I was the only source of water.

What the hell was this? I was so horrified that for a moment I forgot all about the pain. What was he doing and why didn't anyone stop him? Surely my dad should be on his feet by now, dragging him off me and punching him for assaulting his little princess (in public no less). I looked across at him for help but he seemed much more interested in his pork pie than this old pervert munching away on his daughter. Why didn't somebody do something?

I don't know how long this assault lasted but it seemed like hours until Jim let go of me, he turned away, spat in the sand (disgusting) then clapped me on the back and went back to his sandwiches. My mother appeared with a plaster, stuck it over the stinging bit and then told me to say thank you to Jim. What? I was supposed to be grateful for that, what was going on here? Suddenly I didn't know which one of our families was the strangest.

All the way home I was still in shock, I couldn't wait to get out if this car and away from these people with their betrayals and weird habits. I couldn't understand why nobody was mentioning anything. This was the most shocking thing that had ever happened to me and they were all acting like it was nothing. I didn't know what was going on but I knew I never wanted to see Miriam or the rest of her family ever again.

Luckily, I didn't have to wait too long to get my wish. A couple of weeks later my dad went round to Miriam's to do some wallpapering for her (ha, serve her right). Jim was busy at work so he didn't have the time to do it. After a couple of hours my dad came back looking very shocked, he practically threw his tools through the door before him. My mother looked up startled, what could be wrong? They both disappeared into the kitchen where I could hear muffled whispering before I heard my mother shout:

"She did what?!"

I was intrigued, what on earth could have caused such a commotion? I found out a few days later by listening at the door when my mother was talking to Aunty Dolly. Apparently, while my dad was up his ladders tackling a particularly tricky bodge-up, Miriam had come up beside him and put her hand on his leg.

He was mortified, he had been sexually harassed.

Hah, call that sexual harassment. Come and see me when you've had some weirdo giving you an unexpected love bite in the middle of a crowded beach while your father gives more attention to his pork pie than you and you're only five.

It wasn't until the next year that all this made sense. We were all watching Skippy the Bush Kangaroo on the telly, somebody had gone wandering in the outback and had been bitten by a snake. Some other bloke started sucking the poison out of this poor man's leg to save his life, while Skippy hopped off to get help.

"Oh look." said my mother "That's what Jim did to you last year to get the bee sting out."

Was it? This was news to me. Why did nobody bother to explain this at the time? It might have been helpful. So, Jim wasn't such a weirdo after all he had only been trying to help, and he wasn't spitting because he was disgusting, he was getting rid of the bee sting. You would have thought that someone might have considered sharing this information with me wouldn't you? I had been having hateful thoughts about him for nothing.

It still didn't change the fact that his wife was a two-faced back stabber who would betray a person just to get a laugh though. My dad had a lucky escape.

After the incident on the ladder Miriam was dead in our house, she never darkened our doorstep again and if we passed her in the street my mother would stick her nose in the air and drag me past her. I just hoped she wasn't spreading the gossip about my little accident around the neighbours, they had enough ammunition already.

Over the years my mother made various friends from round and about. None of them lasted very long, they all went the way of Miriam and those who had come before her. My mother just couldn't help herself, she had a knack of insulting people without even trying. It was never her fault though, it was everyone else that was difficult.

It wasn't until she was well into her sixties that she began to make proper friends, she started going ballroom dancing at the community centre with a lot of ladies in their seventies. While she was concentrating on her moves she didn't talk so that probably helped a bit. For the next ten years or so, every Wednesday afternoon saw her doing the foxtrot bust to bust with Kitty, Peggy and Doris.

CHAPTER FIFTEEN

Rewind That Bit and Start Again

As I seem to have spent a lot of time talking about my mother and all her special little ways I think I should talk a bit about my dad. I have already explained about his skills as a decorator but there was more to him than that.

I already mentioned how he was really shy, he only came out of his shell in front of other people when he'd had a few pints. Then you wanted him to get back in it really quickly. He was a happy drunk, well more silly than happy, well more stupid than silly. One Christmas, he had been for his usual pre-dinner trip to the pub with my uncle and came home to find me doing the washing up. He crept up behind me, grabbed me by the neck and shoved me head first into the sink.

My first thought as the bubbles rushed up my nose was that it must be my mother giving me this unexpected bath but this was a new one even for her. My dad thought it was hilarious and stood there giggling like a schoolboy. He carried on laughing even after I emptied a pan of soapy water over his head. Unfortunately, my mother wasn't so amused and we both got into trouble.

When I was little the kids in our street loved him, they would come and call for him to play out and he would go off and play football in the street with them. He also played on a weekend for a grown-up team and he was always coming home with his legs pouring with blood from where the other players had kicked him. My mother would fetch the washing up bowl full of warm water and Dettol and we would spend half an hour cleaning him up and sticking plasters on him. My mother must have felt like she had two kids.

He had met my mother when they were both fifteen and just leaving school. He was eating an apple on the corner of the street and she went by and pinched it off him, you would think that would have set alarm bells ringing but if it did he never heard them. They started 'courting' and from what I can make out they spent the next three years on their bikes. All their early photos are of them on bikes, they would cycle for miles every weekend with their friends. This was before they discovered their love of walking everywhere for no apparent reason. I think they did so much cycling to get away from my nanna who never really took to my mother. In her defence, I don't think any woman would have been good enough for my dad though, not even royalty. They courted until they were eighteen and then my dad was called up for National Service and sent abroad for two years. They wrote all the time, well my mother wrote long letters while my dad sent home postcards from all the places he'd been. Each one came with a description of what he had eaten in all these various places, he was such a romantic. He also sent lots of photos home and from what I've seen most of his time over there was spent sitting outside bars drinking beer with his shirt off.

One photo that used to have pride of place on our sideboard was of him in his uniform holding his rifle, I used to think he was a Red Indian because of the big feather sticking up at the back of his cap. I found out when I was older that it wasn't a feather, he was standing in front of a palm tree.

Anyway, when he had done his bit he came home and proposed to my mother. This went down like a lead balloon with my nanna and she flatly refused to give her permission for the wedding. In those days, you had to be twenty-one to get married. This didn't deter them and they tied the knot the day after my dad turned twenty-one. They had a church wedding and my nanna attended under protest, you can easily pick her out on the photos because she's the one with the face like a smacked arse.

My dad seemed to be really close to his father who was actually his stepfather. He had been brought up by my nanna on her own for a while after his real father died. He later found out that my nanna had been a bit economical with the truth. It came out one day that he had actually been born nine years after his real father died. It turned out that his step father was actually his real father and his name was on the birth certificate of both my dad and his sister my Aunty Dolly. He and my nanna had been together for years and were just waiting for his wife to pop her clogs before they could get married. This made my nanna look like a bit of a hypocrite when she found out that Aunty Dolly was expecting out of wedlock and would have to get married. She had a complete hissy fit and said she would never be able to hold her head up in the street. A clear case of pot and kettle.

I think my mother was really brave to move into my nanna's house, she even spent her wedding night there with my nanna and granddad in the next room. There was no honeymoon or anything, they were married on the Saturday and both back at work on the

Monday. If I was my mother I would have slept with one eye open for the whole time I lived there.

They settled down to married life and eventually moved in next door as I have already mentioned. Four years later I came into the picture, making my dad's life complete and providing my mother with endless entertainment. From the beginning, it seemed like I had been sent as a playmate for my dad. We played board games, football, and just about lived on the playground, he even played dolls with me and I have vivid memories of putting rollers and ribbons in his hair.

He spent hours running up and down the street holding onto the back of my bike when my stabilisers came off and on Saturday afternoons we wrestled. I would put on my Robin costume (I preferred him to Batman) and we would throw each other around the living room until my mother came in and shouted at us for making a mess and squashing the dog. He was never too tired to play even when he'd been at work all day. I would wait at the door for him every night and at bedtime I'd lie awake for ages worrying myself sick that he might die and leave me alone with my mother. The thought of him not being there terrified me, as you can see I was a cheerful child.

My parents always seemed to be quite different from the rest of their respective families, it was as if they were meant to find each other. They both had the same strange ideas about life and over the years their individual strangeness began to merge until they both believed the same nonsense. One example of this was my mother's belief that you could get a sun tan without any sign of the sun. To this day, she is adamant that all you need for a good tan is the wind. She has been preaching this idea for years, never noticing the sniggers from everyone she tells. I try to tell her that if this was true we would have heard about it on the telly by now but she swears it is a stone-cold fact. Every time the weather gets bad and we have gale force winds I point out to her the lack of people in bikinis lining the streets but to no avail. She will not be wrong.

Another one of my parent's little gems was priceless and they lived by this code for years. Nobody could convince them that they were wrong, it was,

'Always Take the Highest Estimate!'

They were a salesman's dream come true, in their minds if you chose the lowest estimate you were getting ripped off. If it was too cheap there must be something wrong and so to get the best for your money you should always go with the person who wanted to charge you the most money. How could you argue with that?

All my life I heard stories from my mother about my dad's terrible temper. Apparently, he didn't lose it often but when he did you'd better watch out, it was terrifying and it could take three grown men to hold him back once he got going. This sounded nothing like the dad I knew. The way she told it she made him sound like the Hulk, although she never mentioned anything about him turning green. I think she must have been slightly exaggerating because until the day he died I never saw my dad anything but mildly annoyed. God knows my mother gave him enough reasons to blow a fuse but he always remained really easy going. One afternoon after I had grown up and left home my mother was sexually assaulted by the pensioner next door. My dad's response to this was to avoid eye contact with him over the fence when they were both out doing the gardening.

If the thought of your wife rolling around the carpet trapped underneath the randy old goat from next door didn't get your dander up, I don't know what would. If I had been my mother I would have been quite insulted.

It seemed to me that he went through his whole life trying to avoid confrontation. He would never complain about anything, no matter how bad the service, if we were ever in a café and there was something wrong with his meal he would never say anything. They could have brought his dinner crawling with maggots and he would have eaten it politely rather than cause a scene.

He used to tell me if anyone ever upset me I should just walk away with my head held high and ignore them, they weren't worth it and they were just jealous because I was better than them. I tried this couple of times but it didn't work, I just got beaten up for acting snobby.

He seemed very happy with his lot in life and never tried to better himself. He never looked for a better job, he never learnt to drive so we never owned a car. His one goal in life was to get a council house with a back garden and indoor plumbing, he achieved this when I was nine and as far as he was concerned he'd made it. Me and my brother were brought up not to expect much, as long as we got a job and a council house like my dad then we'd done just fine. We were never encouraged to own our own home or possess a car, that wasn't for the likes of us, that was for the people with money. He never figured out that all the rent he was paying over the years could just as easily be paying off a mortgage.

Eventually Maggie Thatcher brought in the right to buy your council house scheme and he became a home owner. It was more than he ever dreamed of, he bought a greenhouse to put up in the garden he now owned and spent the rest of his days pottering about in it.

The one thing that set my dad apart from everyone else I ever knew was his ability to rewrite his own history (as well as mine). He got my mother on board with this early on and the pair of them stuck to it their whole lives, in fact my mother still does it on a daily basis. If anything happened in their lives that they weren't happy with they would simply edit it out and replace it with something more fitting. Whole chunks of their life would be wiped out, events, places, people, all torn from the pages of their history as if they had never existed in the first place.

Even stranger though was that afterwards they would convince themselves that the new version was the truth and they would stick to it come hell or high water. It didn't matter if other people had been there and knew what really happened, they would stick to their guns and wouldn't budge. It drove people mad, especially my Aunty Dolly.

You could have strapped them to the most advanced lie detector known to man and they would both pass with flying colours. My mother would even go as far as inventing completely new non- existent people to fit in with these tales. It was as if they had a vision of the perfect family and perfect life and anything that spoiled their vision was instantly wiped out. They couldn't deal with anything bad happening so they flatly refused to face it. They didn't just bury their heads in the sand, they dug a bloody big pit, jumped in and then got someone to fill it in after them.

All their lives they worried about what people would think, it was their worst fear to be thought of as not as good as everyone else. They never got that by carrying on in this way they were making people think they were lunatics.

It would have been bad enough if they had just told their tales to friends and acquaintances who weren't very close but they told their stories to close friends, family, and even me, who had actually been there.

I had been present at most of the pre-edited events but they still included me in their made for TV versions and tried to convince me it was the truth. I refused to go along with all this nonsense but they chose to ignore that as well, it was infuriating. They got my brother involved in their madness from an early age and after a while he started doing it too. It's lucky I left home at a young age and never got infected otherwise this story would read like Mary Poppins, only without any sad bits.

I have lost count of the times I have been accosted by bewildered relatives demanding to know about things they'd just heard from my mother. When did this happen and why hadn't they heard about it? They all came to realise eventually that everything was in my parent's imagination and from then on took the mickey out of them mercilessly. It didn't matter though, my parents just edited that out as well.

My mother is still carrying on this madness fifty years later, most of her life has been completely rewritten to resemble an afternoon movie for Channel 5. Even after my dad died she changed most of the circumstances so that his passing would fit in better with how she thought it should be. I like to think he would have been proud of her for that.

CHAPTER SIXTEEN

Secrets and lies

It was early in 1969 and I was eight years old when things got a bit weird. Well more weird than usual really, it started with two things...

Firstly, my mother began to get a bit fatter, I had noticed her struggling to do up the zip on her skirt and it looked as though she couldn't fasten her coat properly. She was no longer working at the chocolate factory so I was a bit puzzled as to what was going on, I hadn't noticed her eating any more than usual

The second thing was more worrying, my parents had a secret. I knew this because there was a lot of whispering going on in the kitchen. Even when they weren't whispering they would stop talking as soon as I entered the room and look as if they were really interested in the wallpaper. What could be going on? Christmas had only just gone so they couldn't be discussing my presents. If my dad had found out any of my mother's indiscretions there wouldn't be whispering, more likely shouting so that wasn't it. I was flummoxed.

After this had gone on for a couple of weeks it suddenly hit me, I didn't know why I hadn't seen it before it was so obvious. They were getting ready to tell me I was adopted, I had always known deep down that I wasn't really related to these people, I was different. Maybe my real family regretted giving me away and wanted me back. Probably they'd got wind of the clothes, or the haircut, or the Dame Edna glasses or maybe all three. Maybe they'd roll up in their big car and have a right go at my mother for what she'd turned me into before whisking me off to buy new stuff. They would get me some proper clothes, nice glasses and maybe a wig to wear until my hair grew back. They were going to save me.

After I really thought about it I got scared, these parents might be a bit odd but they were the only family I had ever known, I didn't want to go. I couldn't bear the thought of not seeing my dad again (even if he wasn't really mine) and even my adopted mother wasn't awful all the time. What was I going to do? Maybe I could get my real family to leave me here, just give these parents a telling off about my appearance and maybe send me a bit if money every month. After all, in the last eight years they'd never bothered with me, why start now.

I discussed this at length with Johnny as we sat on the swings in the playground. He didn't want me to leave any more than I did, we were a double act. He confessed that he had always felt he was adopted too and had been waiting for someone to turn up and claim him for years. No wonder we had hit it off straight away, we were kindred spirits both abandoned at birth and both unwanted by our real families. Maybe we had met before at the orphanage. I'm starting to see the obvious here, I am blessed with my mother's gift for invention.

Anyway, the next few days went by with no mention of my adoption or impending leaving. I wished they would just hurry up and break it to me, I was on tenterhooks just waiting. Maybe it was time to have a word with my Aunty Dolly again. Then I thought better of it, over the years I had asked her at least three times a year about my being adopted and I think she was getting a bit sick of it. She always told me the same story, that she had been there when I was born and that I hadn't been swapped for another baby. As final proof, she would point out that I still had the same birthmark on my bum that she had seen just minutes after I was born. Maybe she was in on it with the rest of them.

The next week with still no news from either set of parents I was walking home from school with my mother. One of the women from our street stopped her and they were gassing away while I stood minding my own business. All of a sudden, this woman asked her when the baby was due and my ears pricked up. What baby was this? Was I being swapped for a younger model already? My mother looked down at me and said it was time I was told, I was getting a little brother or sister soon. This explained a lot, I hadn't even considered this although when you looked at my knowledge of the birds and the bees it wasn't surprising. Oh, the relief, I wasn't being sent away, maybe Aunty Dolly was telling the truth and I really did belong here.

"Is that what you and my dad were whispering about all the time?" I asked her.

"Yes." she said "We didn't want to tell you yet until we were sure about it."

I wasn't really sure what to say then, do you offer your own mother congratulations or what?

In the end, I asked if it was ok to tell people about it and she said yes it wasn't a secret now, then she gave me a couple of pennies to get some sweets from the corner shop.

"Can I tell Sylvie and Alan?" I asked, they were the couple who owned the shop. My mother said yes that was fine and so off I went, full of self-importance with my news. I had seen men on the telly announce that they were getting a baby, they always got slapped on the back and given a cigar. I didn't mind being slapped that much (I was used to that) but I didn't fancy a cigar. Maybe they would give me a jelly snake for free instead, surely when they heard my good news my money would be no good in their shop.

I burst through the door and into the shop, Alan and Sylvie were both there with a couple of customers and Alan looked up and waved at me. It wasn't a conventional wave, you see he only had a thumb and a few little stumps where his fingers used to be. In his younger days, he had worked in a saw mill and I don't think he was all that good at his job. Still, he didn't seem to miss his fingers and he was always happy in his work although Sylvie always looked slightly alarmed when he was using the bacon slicer. Anyway, I rushed up to the counter to deliver my earth-shattering news.

"My mam's having a baby" I blurted out proudly, waiting for the cheers and offers of free sweets. I was to be sadly disappointed, Sylvie practically dragged me over the counter.

"You shut your big mouth you dirty little gossip" she hissed.

"Spreading your mother's private business all over the street, you should be ashamed of yourself."

Well this wasn't the reaction I was expecting, how dare she talk to me like that. The other women in the shop were sniggering at me and I could feel my face going bright red. Gathering my dignity I took my two penny pieces and left hurriedly, if they thought I was going to give them my money now they were very much mistaken. I would buy my jelly snakes and blackjacks elsewhere from now on.

I went home and told my mother about the awful treatment I had suffered. She said she'd put them straight but it didn't matter, I could still tell everyone at school. That would have to do then but I still didn't want to go back into that shop, that was no way to treat one of your best customers. When I thought of how much I had spent in there over the years as well, especially during my clumsy period.

My next stop was Johnny's house to tell him the big news. He was relieved to find out I wasn't going to be taken away by my real family and we discussed the possibility that maybe I had been wrong all these years and I wasn't adopted after all. I asked him why he thought he wasn't with his real family and he said it was because he didn't look like either of his parents. His mother and father were normal sized people while he, even at nine years old would have trouble squeezing into his dad's clothes. I pointed out to him that his mother feeding him seven square meals a day could have something to do with this, he had to agree with me there. Also, if another family did ever turn up to claim him they would never be able to prise him away from Mrs S. She would die before she would let anyone take her baby boy away from her. I think he felt better by the time I left him to finish his third helping of dinner.

When my dad came home that night he was delighted to find out that I knew what was going on.

He said he had been dying to tell me because he didn't like keeping secrets.

"You and me both mate." I thought, some of us had no choice.

Anyway, we had a good laugh picking names to annoy my mother, I said if it was a girl we should call her Dolores after Aunty Dolly but my dad said no, she should definitely be called Ada after his mother. This didn't go down at all well with my mother who didn't see the funny side at all. When I suggested if it was a boy we should call him Julian or Dick after the Famous Five she said it was time I went to bed.

The next morning at school I told everyone my news. None of them were really all that bothered, most of them had brothers and sisters and didn't see what the big deal was. I supposed, to them it was all perfectly normal. Some of them came from big families with loads of kids, my friend Carol who lived backway to us had eleven brothers and sisters. I couldn't imagine how they all fitted in their little house or where they all slept. They only had two proper bedrooms and a small box room the same as us. Her mother was a tiny little thing, most of her kids were bigger than her, even the young ones. She kept them all in line though and could often be seen rounding them all up with her big sweeping brush. My mother said she kept a box next to the sink so she could stand on it to scrub their necks before bedtime.

The next few months passed quite quickly. My mother got steadily bigger and none of her clothes would fit her any more. I kept hearing people tell her she was eating for two now but by the size of her she was eating for four. She had a craving for Pontefract

Cakes, little round flat circles of liquorice and she ate them by the ton. My dad said this baby was going to come out round, flat and black which I found this quite alarming. She began wearing enormous smocks in bright yellows and pinks which made her look like she was part of a three-piece suite. I was starting to worry about how big this baby was going to be. I wondered if this what Johnny's mother had looked like, he said she'd told him he was a big baby.

Another strange thing was that she seemed to be in a good mood most of the time now, I hadn't been taught a good lesson in ages. Mind you she was so big now I doubt she could have chased me round the coffee table if she'd wanted to. Even if she did she would stop half way through for something to eat.

I was still in the dark about this whole baby thing. I had figured out by now that babies weren't brought in a black bag by the doctor, I had proof of that in front of me. What I didn't know was how it had got in there in the first place, and how the hell was it going to get out. Every time I tried to bring up the subject my parents seemed to develop coughing fits and find urgent things to attend to in another room. One day when I wouldn't let the matter drop and followed my mother from room to room waiting for her to stop coughing she muttered something about it growing from a seed in her tummy.

I was extremely worried by this, I was very fond of eating grapes and I didn't always spit the pips out, they were seeds weren't they. Good grief this wasn't going to happen to me was it? I was in no position to have a baby, I couldn't even keep track of my dolls. I was always getting told off for leaving them in the backyard and dropping them down the hole in my playroom where they would re-emerge seconds later in the pantry. Usually I saved this feat for transvestite Action Man/Sindy. My friend Denise had told me once that if you swallowed apple pips you would grow an apple tree in your belly. I didn't always believe the things she told me but by that logic I would be more likely to be growing a grape vine than a baby, wouldn't I?

I asked my cousin Janice about all this the next day when I went for a visit, they had all moved to a new house a couple of years ago, and now lived miles away. I only got to see them weekends and school holidays now so I had to wait longer for my sponge and custard fix. Anyway, when I told her of my worries she fell about laughing. She was thirteen now so she was practically an adult, she told me that no you couldn't get pregnant from eating grapes. She said you needed a husband to get a baby then she said sometimes you could manage it without a husband but that would get you talked about and pointed at in the street like that woman at number six. Then she clammed up and told me I wasn't old enough to understand yet.

I was more baffled than ever, why wouldn't someone just tell me the truth? I wished I could remember more of the nonsense Margaret Dobbs had been telling me last year, a lot of what I could remember was starting to ring true now. Even so she had never bothered to tell us how the baby got out, she was too wrapped up in the process of how it got in there in the first place. I had a feeling she was going to end up like that woman at number six.

In the end, I decided to give up asking questions, it wasn't getting me anywhere and anyway surely I'd see for myself soon, my mother only had a couple of months to go. I'd been told that when the time came my dad would take my mother off to the hospital and I would go and stay with Aunty Dolly until it was all over. I had been born at home so I didn't see why she had to go to hospital for this one but as usual when I asked why this was I was just given the runaround. They said that things were different now to when I had been born and that's just how it was. Good god they made it sound like I had been born in the olden days.

A couple of weeks later we went on holiday to my Uncle and Aunty in Derbyshire. My uncle was my mother's older brother but he seemed a lot more normal than she was, whatever had happened in their family it seemed only my mother was affected. I had often quizzed their only daughter (my cousin) but she was adamant that she had never been publicly humiliated or used as a beggar in her neighbourhood. We were to stay with them for a week so that my parents could have a break before they had to start with all the baby stuff. Apparently, there was a lot of night feeding involved with a baby. Didn't seem like much of a change there, there was a lot of night feeding involved with my mother.

My Uncle came through to pick us up in his car. It was about a two-hour journey and that could sometimes turn into three hours depending on how car sick I got. Usually I was given a bucket and told to just get on with it but my mother couldn't stand the smell of vomit in her delicate state so we had to keep stopping so they could drag me to the side of the road.

Eventually we arrived and got ourselves settled in for the week. My Aunty and Uncle lived in the countryside which to my parents usually meant endless walking, usually dragging mountains of sandwiches with us. This visit though my mother was incapable of not much more than a slow shufflle around the house. By this time she was huge, I was starting to think that my little brother or sister was going to be bigger than me.

Anyway, one morning after we'd been there for about three days me and my dad and my uncle and cousin all set off for a walk through the village leaving my mother with my aunty for company. We hadn't gone very far when a big white van screeched up beside us, the driver shouted something I didn't hear to my uncle and we were all bundled into the van. Now what was going on, was this a kidnapping? There couldn't be much of a ransom demand for our family. It turned out the kidnapper was a neighbour of my uncle who had been sent to look for us, something had gone on back at the house. We pulled up outside the house and me and my cousin were shoved unceremoniously out onto the pavement where my aunty was waiting for us. Then the van took off again with my dad and my uncle still inside.

When we got in the house my Aunty explained that my mother thought the baby was coming early so she'd rung for an ambulance and they'd taken her off to the local hospital. We then had a long wait for my dad to get back. When he returned a few hours later he told us that my mother had to stay in for a few days and rest because they didn't want the baby to get here too early

This few days turned into ten, we couldn't go home and leave my mother so our holiday got extended. I was bored sick, every day my dad would visit the hospital and because kids weren't allowed in I had to wait in the car park and wave to my mother through a little window on the top floor. I just wanted to go home, this bloody baby was disrupting my life before it even got here. As if I didn't have enough to put up with already. I couldn't see why it was in such a rush to get here, if it knew what was waiting on the outside it should be hanging on in there for grim death.

Eventually the hospital let my mother out and my uncle shoved us all in the car and took us home. I think the family were glad to see the back of us really, they hadn't planned on us staying for two weeks and for my uncle to spend every day driving backwards and forwards to the hospital. I noticed he seemed to be driving a lot faster going home than he had done on the way there and I was back to clutching a bucket between my knees instead of him pulling over every few miles. I think he was terrified my mother would go into labour again and he'd be forced to turn around and take us back for another fortnight.

The closer we got to our home the more he seemed to relax, by the time we reached our town he was whistling. When we arrived home, he helped my dad in with the bags and then he was off, he didn't even stay for a cup of tea. My dad said he was just glad his offspring wasn't going to be born outside Yorkshire.

It was the summer holidays so I was still off school. I went back to normal, playing out every day with my friends. The only difference was I wasn't allowed to leave our little street, I had to stay within earshot of my mother in case anything happened. She was spending every day laying down with her feet up, trying to keep the baby from making its appearance until she was ready. When I asked her why it couldn't come now she said it would be too small, looking at the size of her belly I thought she must be wrong there.

We had been home for a couple of weeks when there was a bit of a panic. My mother was going into hospital and I was being sent to stay at Aunty Dolly's for a few days. It seemed that this baby wasn't prepared to wait much longer and it was determined to make an appearance soon. I didn't mind, I loved staying at Aunty Dolly's, colour telly and all the sponge and custard I could eat. I would even put up with Malcom who had grown a bit bored with judo and was into his Chinese burn phase. For the next few days my arms would be decorated with lovely red stripes, he was fifteen now, it really was time he outgrew all this torture.

There were no spare beds at Aunty Dolly's so I had to 'top and tail' with Janice. I always had to sleep with my head at the bottom of the bed and she would warn me every night not to fart. Cheek, I had to sleep with her bony feet in my face and I never complained. Janice was very much into George Best in those days and every inch of her wallpaper was covered with pictures of him. I would wake up every morning with ninety pairs of eyes watching me, it was creepy.

After a couple of days my dad turned up and told me I had a baby brother. He told me to pack my bags, he was taking me home and later on he would take me to visit my mother and my new baby brother.

It was the end of an era. I was an only child no longer.

CHAPTER SEVENTEEN

Happy Families

My introduction to my new brother was a little strange. On the telly and in films every time I had seen people visiting a new mother everything was lovely. The new mum would be sitting up in bed in a lovely room surrounded by beautiful flowers and cards. She would be wearing a pretty nightgown with optional matching bed jacket and her hair and makeup would be perfect. She would be smiling serenely while in her arms she cradled a perfect, chubby, sweet smelling little cherub, sleeping peacefully swaddled in soft blankets. The family would gather round the bed gazing fondly at the new-born who would be passed to the older children so they didn't feel left out. Everything was perfect.

This was our family so I wasn't expecting it to be exactly like that, I was being realistic but it was so far away from that it was laughable (now).

We entered the maternity hospital and my dad took me to the ward my mother was on. Instead of being in a lovely private room my mother was on a ward full of other new mothers. It smelt of dirty nappies and disinfectant and wasn't very tidy. We had to walk right down to the bottom of the ward to find my mother's bed passing all the other women in their beds. I never expected that so many women would be having babies at once.

We got to the end of the ward, my dad pulled back a curtain and there was my mother. Instead of sitting up smiling with her arms outstretched in greeting she was hunched under the blankets. Her head was sticking out of the covers, hair all over the place and she was scowling. Oh god the madwoman was back, I hadn't seen her for a few months and it caught me off guard. Why hadn't my dad warned me? I looked up at him puzzled but he shot me back a look that said "Act normal and don't say anything."

My mother heaved herself up in the bed, grunted hello and asked if we'd brought anything to eat, then she got stuck into the chocolates we'd brought. I noticed that whatever she'd had for dinner she'd spilt down her nightie.

I was looking around for my brother but I couldn't see him anywhere, I hoped she wasn't sitting on him. When she'd had a few more coffee creams she told me he was in the special nursery where the small babies had to stay so the nurses could look after them. I could go and see him soon through a window on the way out. We chatted for a bit while my dad fiddled around with his tie and hummed a lot, he wasn't very good at small talk. My mother said she hoped I was behaving myself and I assured her I was being a model citizen, no point in annoying her any more than was necessary.

After what seemed like hours the bell sounded to announce the end of visiting hours and me and my dad nearly fell over each other in our hurry to leave. We kissed my mother goodbye, my dad said he'd be back tomorrow and then we tried to get through the doors alongside all the other visitors who were fighting to get away.

On the way out my dad said now he'd take me to see my brother. He led me down a few corridors to the nursery where a tired looking nurse asked which baby we'd come to see. My dad told her and she disappeared through a door. A few minutes later she was at the big window holding what looked like a small rag doll wrapped in a blanket. She offered this bundle up to the glass so we could get a better look and that's how I finally got to meet my brother. He was smaller than my dolls at home, a little red wrinkled thing. He reminded me of a baby rat I'd seen on Animal Magic on the telly. I didn't really know what to say but after racking my brain for a few minutes I came up with the only thing I could think of,

"Are you sure that's the right one?"

I couldn't imagine how my mother could have been so enormous and yet only produce this little scrap of a thing.

My dad assured me this was my brother and pointed to the name tag around his leg, I could have pointed out that mistakes could be made but thought better of it. Wanting to be polite I introduced myself and told my new brother I would see him on my next visit, then we pulled a few silly faces through the glass and waved goodbye to him. The nurse went off to put him back in his cupboard or wherever it was they kept him and we went home, stopping off on the way for fish and chips. That would have annoyed my mother no end.

For the next few days it was just me and my dad, whenever he went back to the hospital he left me next door at Johnny's house. The hospital didn't like children visiting which seemed a bit stupid really when half the population in there was under a week old. One day while my dad was away visiting the rest of his family Mrs S took me and Johnny to a carnival at the park. We went on a few game stalls, Johnny won a big teddy and I won a goldfish in a plastic bag. He wanted to swap but I said no, I wanted a pet. He pointed out that I could give the teddy to the new baby and I would look like I was a good sister. I thought about it for a second but no, I wanted a goldfish and besides I'd already named him Goldie (very original).

When we got home my dad was back, I presented him with my prize and he dug around in the back of the pantry until he found an old goldfish bowl, there had been a few Goldie's in my life. We plonked him in it and put the bowl in pride of place on top of the telly. Over tea, my dad told me that my mother was coming home tomorrow but my brother would have to stay in hospital for a few more weeks until he put enough weight on to come home. He only weighed four pounds, nowadays that wouldn't matter but back then it was a dangerous weight. They had no idea then that in another twenty years or so a baby weighing only one pound could survive.

He told me that for the next few days I was to be on my best behaviour and should try to be as helpful as I could to my mother. On no account should I do anything to annoy her as she was feeling a bit depressed and might seem a bit snappy. I didn't know how I was going to avoid annoying her, it didn't take much. Sometimes just walking into the same room was enough to set her off. I promised him I'd be helpful and behave. Luckily he had a week off work so I wouldn't be left on my own, I had back up.

The next afternoon my dad set off to pick up my mother, they arrived home in a taxi about an hour later. I had made my mother a welcome home card, trying to get off on the right foot. When she was brought in and seated on the couch I presented it to her proudly, she glanced at it and said thank you it was very nice. So far so good. I was just setting the card up on the mantelpiece for her when she let out an ear-splitting shriek, I almost swallowed my gobstopper whole, she had caught me completely off guard. My dad flew in from the kitchen with a look that said

"Now what have you done?"

I didn't have a clue. We soon found out though, she had spotted Goldie minding his own business on top of the telly.

"What the hell is that filthy thing doing in my house?" she raged "I will not have dirty, stinking animals in my front room."

With that she burst into tears and fled into the kitchen. I thought that was a bit over dramatic, it was only a goldfish. It wasn't as if he was going to run riot round the front room chewing the furniture and peeing on the carpet.

I didn't have any idea about post- natal depression, I don't think anyone else had either in those days. Looking back, I can see it must have been awful for her to go through everything she had and still come home without her baby. She should have been bonding with him but he was miles away being fed and looked after by strangers. I will make allowances for this but not for the rest of it.

We quickly settled into a routine after she came home. Every afternoon she would take me on the bus to the hospital where we would spend a couple of hours with my brother. She was allowed to hold him and feed and change him, she showed me how to change his nappy but I was not impressed at all. It wasn't just the gunk that came out of him although that was bad enough, I had no idea that they fed mushy peas to babies. It was also the fact that I was completely unfamiliar with boy's bits, I had never seen anything like it. At first I thought he must be deformed but nobody was mentioning it, maybe that's why my mother had been so upset, there was something wrong with him. Then on my way to the toilet one day I came across another mother changing her baby and lo and behold he had the same deformity. I silently thanked my parents, another thing they'd kept me in the dark about.

It was now September and time for me to go back to school. My mother kept up the hospital visiting without me, she came home every day and told me how much bigger my brother was getting. Eventually three weeks later she was allowed to bring him home.

There was much excitement that day, my dad took the day off work to go with my mother to the hospital and soon after all three of them arrived back in a taxi. My mother was right, my brother was a lot bigger than when I'd last seen him but he was still really tiny. He was plonked into his carry cot which promptly swallowed him up. Almost immediately the nosy neighbours started descending on us, one by one they came in and peered into the carry cot, making cooing noises. I realised they were all giving him money, pressing it into his little hand for luck.

These were the same neighbours that clutched their purses to their pinnies and did a runner when they saw me coming up the street. They'd avoided me like the plague for years and now here they were throwing money at my brother like none of it had ever happened. What about me, where was my reward?

This went on for the first two or three days, it was amazing. They kept coming, all wittering on about giving him good luck as they shoved silver coins at him. He had no idea what money was, he couldn't even see further than the end of his nose yet he had made more in the last three days than I'd had in the last three years. He had a jar on the mantelpiece that was filling up at an alarming rate, I couldn't believe how two faced these neighbours were being.

On the third day I had had enough. For the fourth time that day I was patted on the head and asked what it was like to be a big sister,

"Poor" I wanted to say.

I took my leave and went to sit in the other room where I could vent my rage at Goldie who was on death row but hoping for a stay of execution. After a while I began to feel bad for being so mean. When I really thought about it all these people were doing my brother a favour. I could get away and be at school all day but he would be spending the next five years home alone with my mother. He was going to need all the luck he could get.

CHAPTER EIGHTEEN

The Happiest Days

I never liked school. From the day I started primary school at age five to the day I left high school at age fifteen I don't recall a single enjoyable day. I made the best of it and even had some good laughs but I would still rather have been anywhere else, even home some days.

My first teacher was Mrs Williams, she was a nice motherly lady, older than my mother and she made sure we all got lots of cuddles. We didn't do much work in that first year, mostly we played with toys, the classroom was full of them. There was a big play house in the corner with a pretend kitchen, it even had a toy washing machine and mini ironing board with a little pretend steam iron. There was a fridge and an oven and even a little dining table and chairs. Next to the play house was a dressing up area full of dresses, hats, shoes and handbags.

It was a little strange though because there were no boy's toys to speak of. A few Lego bricks but that was all, no guns, no cowboys or Indians, no cars and definitely no Action Man. I knew this for a fact as it's the first thing I looked for during my first forage into the toy box. The boys mostly played in the house and helped out with the housework, looking back I think Mrs Williams might have been a feminist. We all played nicely together though and nobody seemed to think it strange when Kevin Braithwaite did the ironing while wearing a sparkly dress and sandals.

As we were all really young and some of us found leaving our mothers a bit traumatic there were sometimes accidents and our little kitchen floor would develop puddles (luckily, we had a little mop and bucket). When this happened, the culprit would be sent to the staff room where the teachers kept spare pairs of pants for just such occasions. Sometimes some of the more stupid among us would have a worse accident than just a puddle on the floor and then our classroom would develop an aroma that no amount of pretend air freshener could shift.

One afternoon Graham Spooner got caught short and decided if he couldn't make it to the toilet in time the next best place would be in the playhouse. Wouldn't you just know the only thing we didn't have in there was a pretend toilet.

The rest of us were sitting round our tables doing a bit of colouring in that day so the first we knew of this development was when the smell hit. I can still smell it to this day, it was horrific. I don't know what they ate at his house but by the stench wafting around our heads it must have been well past its sell by date. While we were all gagging Mrs Williams was running around flinging open all the doors and windows. Then she went in search of the evidence, it didn't take Miss Marple to figure out that something awful had happened in the play house. The steaming pile of diarrhoea kind of gave the game away. Mrs Williams backed out of the little doorway with one of Kevin's headscarves over her face and began hollering for the caretaker to bring sawdust fast. This was the solution to many an accident, if it was on the floor it got covered in sawdust.

While we waited for him to come running, Mrs Williams tried to get to the bottom (no pun intended) of who had done the dastardly deed, it didn't take long. The rest of the class were practically ripping each other to pieces to avoid standing next to Graham. Meanwhile, he was doing his best to act innocent and mingle in among us, the fact that he still had diarrhoea running down his legs seemed to have escaped him. While Mrs Williams tried her best to get a grip on him without actually touching him poor little Cheryl Shufflebotham (honesty that was her real name) could no longer control her nervous stomach and promptly vomited her last meal (school dinners shepherd's pie,) all over herself and Michael Barwick.

The place descended into chaos then. Everyone was running in different directions trying to avoid slipping in the vomit while at the same time keeping a good distance from Graham who was still protesting his innocence and trying to get away from Mrs Williams. Michael Barwick was sobbing because Cheryl had been sick on his new jumper and Cheryl was busy bringing up her pudding (pink blancmange) to join the shepherd's pie. Into the middle of this nightmare came the caretaker brandishing his bucket of sawdust, when he saw the mess he didn't know where to start. He shouted to Mrs Williams that he was going to need more sawdust, lobbed a bucketful over Cheryl's little accident and ran out again.

Meanwhile, Miss Parker from next door had heard the commotion and come to see what was going on. I think she must have regretted it the minute she took her first breath. She immediately began herding the kids not covered in bodily fluids out into the playground. Cheryl was taken into the corridor and made to sit down with her head between her knees, Michael was parted from his jumper and Graham was finally collared and taken to the toilets to be stripped and washed.

Luckily it was almost half past three so we were allowed to go straight home when our mothers turned up. Nobody could have entered that classroom again that day anyway. I can still picture poor Graham being led off by his mother, anorak on his top half and nether regions covered by a tea towel from our kitchen held in place by a chiffon headscarf from the dressing up box.

It took a good week to get the smell to completely disappear from our classroom. Thankfully the weather was still warm enough to have the windows open all day. Once the weather turned cold and the heating was switched on though you could still detect a faint undercurrent of disinfectant and diarrhoea. From that day on poor Graham was watched like a hawk, every time he set foot in the play house the rest of us would run and tell 'Miss' who would immediately ask him if he needed a poo.

We had to stay at primary school until we were nine when we would be shipped off to Junior school. Over the next four years we would all move up together through the various classes. The higher up the school you got the more violent the teachers would get. We had all been lulled into a false sense of security by lovely, cuddly Mrs Williams and weren't prepared for the levels of violence that we were about to encounter.

It would start when you were six with the odd slap from a bare hand, seven and it would be a ruler. Eight meant the sandshoe and by the time you were getting ready to leave at nine you had progressed to the actual cane. In between the teachers would improvise, using whatever came to hand. They all had one thing in common though, they all enjoyed a good shake.

I was present one day when my friend Denise received this treatment. I didn't know what she'd done but somehow, she managed to upset the Headmistress, Miss Ware. She was a monster, I think she had only become a teacher so that she could get her hands on a limitless supply of children.

She really seemed to enjoy inflicting cruelty, I came out into the corridor one day to find her shaking Denise. She was clutching her by the shoulders while she shook her so violently that it looked like her head was in danger of flying off. Her head was snapping backwards and forwards, dislodging her glasses (she had recently joined my gang) and it was a miracle her neck didn't break. After a few minutes of this shaking Miss Ware gave her an almighty shove and she hit the radiator and bounced off onto the floor. Miss Ware picked her up by her cardigan and swung her round and round by it before letting go so that she went flying off into the wall again.

As she slithered down the wall onto the floor, Miss Ware stepped over her as if she were a piece of garbage and started to walk away. I was staring at Denise, willing her to stay down until the old witch had gone but Denise could never help herself. If she'd only kept quiet it would have been over but she had to go and open her gob.

I'm telling my dad" she shouted to Miss Ware's retreating back.

Well that did it, Miss Ware spun on her heel and came back for round two. By the time she'd finished poor Denise's cardigan looked like it was ten sizes too big and we had to retrieve her glasses from under the trophy cabinet.

"Bring your father" shouted Miss Ware, on her way out,

"I'll give him the same treatment."

She meant it too. I was in no doubt that if Denise brought her dad into school Miss Ware would swing him around by his overalls and shake him until his teeth flew out. She wasn't scared of anyone, psychopaths never are.

Me and Denise walked slowly home together afterwards. She rolled the sleeves up on her cardigan so her mother wouldn't notice that they were almost trailing on the floor and we tried to rearrange the shoulders so she didn't look so much like Quasimodo. I asked her what she had done to upset Miss Ware and she told me she'd been running in the corridor, yep, that would do it.

We both knew that she wouldn't tell her dad, we never told our parents about what went on at school. We lived in fear of them coming in and showing us up, that would have been even worse. Last year Wendy Ashworth's big fat mother had stormed the classroom to have a go at the teacher for slapping Wendy and she still got teased on a daily basis.

I was lucky, I never got to tangle with Miss Ware. I only popped up on her radar once when I had an accident at school (not that sort). I was running in the playground when as usual I fell over my own feet and crashed face first into the wall. I had done a proper job on my face, I was bleeding all over the place. In a panic, I ran to the staff room for help. I knocked on the door, waited for someone to shout 'come in' and opened the door. Immediately there were gasps from inside when the teachers saw the state of me. I got two steps into the room before Miss Ware's shrill tones rang out.

"Get that child out of here now, she's going to get blood on the carpet"

I was ushered out by Mrs Ramsey the nice school secretary, she took me to her little office where she patched me up and gave me a barley sugar, she didn't have any jelly snakes.

I always behaved myself at school but still received smacks, slaps and shoves. For some reason, I always got the blame for something someone else was doing, the first time this happened to me I was about seven. When the first whistle blew in a morning we had to line up with the rest of our class and stay silent. On the second whistle we would march in single lines to our classrooms, it was a bit like the army.

One day after the first whistle I was standing in my line waiting for the sergeant to blow the second whistle. All of a sudden I was startled out of my thoughts by a sharp slap to the back of my legs. The next minute Mr Pocklington was hissing in my ear

"Stop talking in line."

I hadn't even opened my mouth, what did he think I was, a ventriloquist?

This happened more than once, I always got the blame for talking even if I wasn't sitting next to anyone, I started to think somebody in our class had learnt how to throw their voice.

The everyday slaps became part of school life and after the first couple it just became normal and not worth mentioning. Some of the more mental teachers went in for throwing things at you, we had one teacher, Mr Rolfe who had a thing for wooden blackboard erasers. He would be wiping something off the blackboard when someone would make a noise, even a sniff could set him off. He would spin around eraser in hand and launch it at the nearest head, he didn't care if it wasn't the sniffer. Luckily, he wasn't a very good shot and anyway we all became skilled in ducking as soon as we heard anything, if we hadn't there would have been a lot of brain damaged kids in our class.

Nowadays there would be government enquiries, our school would be closed down and we would all be on the news after we had finished in therapy. Then it was just called education and went on in every school in the country.

Another thing that would never be allowed now was doing P.E in your knickers and vest but we all did it. Nobody even thought about shorts or P.E. kits until we went to high school. There we were, rolling around and balancing on upside down benches (no proper equipment at our school) whilst half naked. Trying to do the splits could be really embarrassing for the girls as some of the navy- blue knickers were very baggy in those days. Today we would be in the Sunday papers and the P.E. teachers would be locked up in a segregation unit but again back then it was normal.

Once a week we would have a P.E. lesson where we did nothing but country dancing, this must have looked a real sight. Thirty kids circling left and right and dozy dohing while wearing their underwear. Sometimes it was hard to link arms in the middle of the circle while trying to hold your knickers up at the same time.

Because ours was a really old school we had no school playing field like some of the more modern schools. This meant that every summer when sports day came around the whole school would be put onto a double decker bus and shipped off to another school on the outskirts of town. This school had massive playing fields with real goal posts, white lines and everything, we were awestruck by how much grass there was. We would stay for the whole day until everyone had finished running, jumping and staggering around trying to keep eggs on spoons. We thought it was great, it was another world to us.

Unfortunately, the pupils from this school didn't take kindly to a bus full of "poor kids" using their facilities and they would shout insults at us when they passed. We were no poorer than they were, they were just lucky enough to go to a newer school than ours. We took no notice anyway, it was just so nice to fall over onto soft grass when we fell instead of ripping our knees off on the cement that we played on every day. We looked forward to this day every year and it always passed really quickly.

Another yearly event was the Harvest Festival, this was a really big deal at our school and all the parents were invited to join us to celebrate. We would be asked to bring in food from home to put on the big display in the hall, after the singing was over this food would be divided up into gift boxes and we would be sent off to deliver it to the old people in the community. The poor old buggers must have dreaded it. Every year our mothers would rake out the old tins of stuff that nobody liked from the back of the cupboards. It would be horrible stuff like tinned prunes and hideous flavours of soup. We would fill our boxes with all this crap and go off knocking on doors to patronise the old folk. Some of them would refuse point blank to open their doors, they would pretend to be out even though we could clearly see them through the window. I think a lot of them were getting the same tins of rubbish back that they had given their grandkids to take to the Harvest Festival.

Nobody could say we didn't recycle back then, some of the tins had been doing the rounds for four or five years.

We always seemed to be collecting money for orphans as well at our school, a few times a year we were given books of 'Sunny Smiles' to sell. These were little booklets with about thirty or so different photographs of little orphan kids all smiling (hence the name). The idea was that the person would pick which photo they liked best and donate some money for the orphanage, then they could keep the photo to remind them how generous they'd been.

Looking back it was madness. We were seven years and eight years old and we were being sent off on our own to knock on strangers' doors offering to sell them photos of little kids. The perverts didn't need the internet in those days, we were there to provide all the jolly's instead. People say it was safer back then though, it wasn't. It was the era of the Moors murders, little kids were being murdered back then just as much as they are today, it's just that we had no Sky News then so you only heard of it if it happened in your town.

It's a wonder more of us didn't get bumped off, it was a dangerous life for kids. At any moment you could be taken out by a blackboard eraser or go skipping off to your doom up the path of the neighbourhood psycho clutching your little book of Sunny Smiles.

My mother would often tell me to make the most of my time at school, she would say that schooldays were the happiest days of your life. If that was true, I could only wonder in horror what could be in store for me in later life.

CHAPTER NINETEEN

New Beginnings

When I was eight and a half and my brother was nine months old my parents dropped the bombshell that we were moving. They had been given a council house on the new estate that my Aunty Dolly had moved to a couple of years before, we would be living five minutes away from them again. Poor Aunty Dolly, she couldn't escape my mother. I was devastated, I didn't want to leave my friends especially Johnny and Denise. We had grown up together and we were like family. I didn't want to leave my school either, it was horrible but we all stuck together. I had been with the same classmates since I was five, every year we all moved up together and when we were nine we were all going to be shipped off to the junior school together. I wouldn't know anyone at a new school, my classmates were used to my strange hair, clothes and glasses. What would new people make of me? I would be a laughing stock.

I begged and pleaded with my parents to reconsider but they wouldn't even listen. They were caught up in the excitement of a garden, indoor toilets and a bathroom with a proper bath. Up until then bath nights consisted of sitting in the tin bath in front of the fire, filling it up with hot water from the copper boiler in the kitchen. There was no privacy, if my mother was in a good mood she would arrange the clothes horse around the bath and hang towels on it. If she couldn't be bothered that day, you just had to sit there exposed. Manys the time some neighbour or other would come traipsing in while I sat there, trying desperately to cover my modesty with the bubbles from Mr Matey.

Anyway, when they got the keys they took me to see the new house. I hated it, it was sandwiched in with hundreds of other houses all identical to each other and everything seemed to be grey. The house itself was ok, I would have a bigger bedroom and it would be nice to have a bath without entertaining the neighbours but I still didn't want any part of it.

I had no choice though and it seemed like no time at all until the removal van rolled up and I was saying my goodbyes. I bid farewell to my blood brother Johnny, the first best friend I had ever had. We didn't kiss goodbye or anything, we shook hands and slapped each other on the back and that was it. To this day, I have no idea why we didn't think to keep in touch, neither of us even thought of writing letters and Johnny's dad was a postman.

The furniture was loaded in the back of the van, then me and my parents and brother were squashed into the front. I watched my friends waving until we turned the corner and then that was it, I never saw them again. Even if we hadn't moved away things would soon have changed anyway. One by one families were starting to move to new council houses that were being built. In a couple more years the full street would be demolished and it would all be gone forever.

We arrived at our new house where Aunty Dolly and my cousins were waiting to help us unload the van. Once everything was in I realised that we didn't really have much. The living room looked ok but the dining room was empty, our old table was far too big to fit in the new house so we left it behind. This house didn't feel like home at all and I was desperately homesick already. My dad told me once we got a few more bits and bobs in and he had decorated (oh God) it would feel more like home. I don't think my brother was liking it much either, in our other house he had never cried that much but in this one he screamed the place down all night every night for the next fortnight.

One thing was for sure, the neighbours knew we had arrived!

Even though I was miserable I had one small thing to look forward to. At my old school somehow, we had become so skilled at country dancing we were entered into a competition at the City Hall. We would be competing against lots of other schools from our town. Because I was an integral part of the team (and because they had nobody else) it was decided that I could come back for the day to compete with the rest of the team. I still had another week before I had to start my new school.

It was quite exciting for all of us because for the first time we wouldn't be dancing in our underwear. For some reason the thought of hundreds of under age kids prancing around the City Hall in their knickers and vests didn't seem right, and so we had costumes (sort of). The boys had their school trousers on with white shirts and the girls had white blouses with horrible green and white gingham skirts that the teachers had made from what looked like old tablecloths.

The great day came and I was taken to town to meet up with the rest of my team. I was bundled inside, given my tablecloth to put on and then we had to line up backstage to wait for our big moment. My mother had reminded me of the Christmas play incident with Maureen Feeny and warned me to behave. It was ok though, Maureen Feeny was long gone, she had left to go to another school not long after we were in the big pie together with the other four and twenty blackbirds.

After a few of the other schools had performed it was our turn, we took our places on the stage and the music began. The judges must have been bored silly, we were all doing the same dance to the same music. I don't know how they kept track. Anyway, it all went by in a blur, a few dozy dohs and circle lefts later and it was all over. We took our bows, left the stage and that was it.

We didn't win, we didn't even come close. The teacher said it was my fault because we had lost points when I stopped to pull up my socks. I think the judges had just lost the will to live and picked any old team just so they could get out of there and get to the bar.

Anyway, it was better than usual, pulling up your socks in front of an audience was more upmarket than pulling up your knickers.

I had to leave my schoolmates then for the last time, as a leaving present I was allowed to keep my tablecloth skirt. Good God hadn't that school done enough to me.

After being in my new house for a week it was time to start my new school, I was dreading it. Luckily, I had already made friends with the girl who lived next door to us, her name was Melanie and she lived with her parents, an older brother Richard who was getting ready to leave home and join the Air Force and her sister Susan who was three years older than us. Her mother was very posh compared to us and her dad was a nurse. I had never come across a man who was a nurse before and I worried a bit about what sort of uniform they made him wear. Melanie wasn't going to be in my class but she said she'd walk to school with me and see me at playtime.

I had been awake all night sick with worry about my first day, I had good reason to worry though because my mother was up to her usual tricks. She had decided I needed to make a good first impression and should be dressed smartly. What was called for here was the tablecloth skirt from the country dancing competition, I was more than horrified, I was almost catatonic with fear. What the hell would my new classmates think to this, didn't my mother realise how hateful, spiteful and cruel kids could be?

I spent the final hour before school begging her to let me wear something else but she wouldn't listen. She told me not to be silly and that I looked lovely, then she gave my Dame Edna glasses a final polish and shoved me out the front door. Melanie was just coming out of her house, she tried to hide her shock when she saw me but I could see through her frozen smile. I had seen this expression lots of times before.

At least there was one thing I could do to limit the fallout, I took off my glasses and shoved them in the pocket of my tablecloth. One less thing to get beaten up for. With that done I took a deep breath and headed off to hell.

As predicted, when I was introduced to my new class jaws dropped and I could hear sniggering and whispering from all around. I could practically hear them thinking:

" That's the entertainment provided for the year then."

I was shown to my desk and took my place with as much dignity as I could muster, it wasn't a lot. During the first lesson, I could see the others sneaking peeks at me from behind their books, even the teacher and she really should have known better. I couldn't wait for playtime to see Melanie's friendly face. Strangely though when I did find her she wanted to spend playtime sitting behind the bins, anyone would think she didn't want to be seen with me.

The first couple of weeks were a nightmare, it was just what I had expected really. A few mornings I refused to go and the new neighbours were treated to the sight of my mother in action, screaming blue murder while dragging me by the neck up the street. She always liked to make a good first impression too.

After the first few weeks it got a lot easier, the other kids got used to seeing me and I wasn't so much of a novelty. They had used up all the insults they had by now and had nothing left to give. Also, I had my school uniform now and wore the same as everybody else so they no longer had my colourful wardrobe to keep them entertained. They never found out about my dirty little secret though, every morning after shouting goodbye to my mother I would take off my glasses and stash them in my satchel. Only Melanie knew and she kept my secret, I think that was to protect herself as much as me.

About a month later a new girl joined our class, she was from down south and spoke with a different accent. The other kids thought this the funniest thing ever and put all their energies into mocking her every word. My ordeal was over, I was accepted.

Even though I was now one of them I couldn't bring myself to join in teasing the poor new girl, I knew just what she was going through. Anyway, I knew I was walking a fine line, if word ever got about the hidden Dame Edna glasses I was done for.

CHAPTER TWENTY

Skid marks and Scandal

I only stayed in my new class for a few more weeks after that. It was end of term, the summer holidays were here and after that we would all move up into the juniors. This was still in the same school but in a separate building. We would have our own playground so that we wouldn't have to mix with the little kids and we had classes in upstairs rooms. Unlike primary school we would have different teachers for each subject and would move around the school all day. It all sounded very grown up.

For now though there were six weeks of summer with no school to worry about, I was starting to enjoy living in my new house now and missing my old friends less and less. My dad was in his element now that he had a garden and he spent hours out there, coming in for his tea bent double until he could get the cramps out of his back and stand up straight again. He discovered a hidden talent for gardening, he had always had it but never had anywhere to put it to use. Now the garden was a mass of colour with flowers everywhere. He also started growing vegetables and we would always have fresh veg straight from the garden. He spent hours after tea poring through seed catalogues and gardening magazines, he was in heaven.

Unfortunately, no matter how hard he tried he couldn't find any hidden talent for decorating. I have already covered his lack of skills in this area so there's no point going over it again. It never got any better no matter how hard he tried, still you can't be good at everything.

That summer was a good one. Because our estate was new and had been built on the outskirts of town we were surrounded by fields. This meant we could go and play rounders and football all day long, summers were always hot back then so we all got really brown.

My dad had a trick of his own for getting a good tan, he said he had learned it in the army. He would mix olive oil and vinegar together and then smother us all in it. We would all lay out in our new garden sizzling away from the oil and smelling like a fish and chip shop, it's a wonder we had any skin left. Today's doctors would have heart attacks if they had seen us then cooking away in the eighty-degree sun.

Sometimes Melanie's parents would take their two girls to the seaside and I always went with them. Her dad had a Robin Reliant van like Del Boy's from Fools and Horses only his was white not yellow. Her dad had never passed his driving test as you didn't need to for a three -wheeled car. He rode a moped for a few years before selling it and deciding he should start driving other people around. Because he had never driven a car in his life before it could get a bit scary. He drove as if he was still by himself on a bike and he would try and slip in among busy traffic. His wife used to slap him with her crossword magazine when he got too carried away.

We were mostly unaware of how close to death we came as we were all squashed in the back among the windbreaks and picnic tables and we had no windows to see out of. All we knew was that any given moment you could find yourself lying on your back, legs in the air and wearing a deck chair on your head.

One day a few weeks into the holidays my mother blackmailed me into taking my brother out in his pram, Melanie and Susan were with me. My brother's pram was enormous, it was a proper big old fashioned thing with big wheels. We pushed him round the block a few times and then I decided to take him up the hill next to the high- rise flats around the corner. In hindsight, I never should have taken a big pram like that up a hill, all was going well until we started to come down again. The hill was quite steep and at the bottom the only thing that separated you from the busy road was a little white fence about a foot tall. The pram was starting to get away from me on the way back down and I was nearly running to keep up. I turned to shout for the others to help me and that's when it happened, I tripped over something (probably my own feet) and went flying, letting go of the pram.

It went hurtling down the hill without me, picking up speed as it went with my brother screaming his head off. I froze, petrified of what was happening in front of me. The other two went charging down the hill after the pram but there was no way anyone could get to it in time. It reached the bottom, hit the little fence and tipped over with my brother still strapped into it. Oh my god what had I done? I had killed my baby brother and I could never go home again. In a blind panic, I turned around and headed off the other way as fast as I could, I would go to my Aunty Dolly's, she would protect me. In my head, I was already seeing myself behind bars, all my old friends would see me on the front of the paper, my life was over.

Then in the distance I became aware of Susan and Melanie shouting at me.

"Come back its ok, he's not dead."
Could it be true, was he really alright? I turned around and started to make my way back down the hill. They were right, he was fine there wasn't a mark on him, he was snivelling a bit now but even that stopped when Melanie gave him a bit of her Milky Way. We took him out of the pram and Susan checked him over, she was in the St Johns Ambulance Brigade so she knew what she was doing. He was perfectly ok, he couldn't walk but he hadn't been able to walk anyway, he was a late developer.

I couldn't believe I'd got away with this one, the only evidence of the near- death experience was a tiny dent on the corner of the pram. I figured if I parked it at the right angle in the hallway my mother wouldn't notice it. By the time she did she might think she'd done it herself, it was a bit of a struggle getting it in and out every day.

After I'd finished shaking and my legs felt normal again we made our way back. My brother was acting perfectly normal, even laughing when Susan played peek a boo with him. I took him back inside and told my mother we were back, I was waiting for her to notice something was up but she didn't seem to notice anything amiss. She got my brother out of the pram and took him off for his dinner.

The next few days I couldn't settle and I watched my brother like a hawk waiting for him to start turning black and blue. How would I explain it if he did? Every time my mother changed his nappy or bathed him I would be hovering in the background looking for any sign of injury. He never showed the slightest sign that anything had happened, it's a good thing he was a late talker or he could have really dropped me in it.

Even when he did start talking he didn't seem to remember anything as far as I could tell. He never pointed at his pram and said:

"Bang" or anything like that.

It did worry me for a while that it took so long for him to start talking, maybe I had given him brain damage or stunted his development. I think he came out of it ok though, nowadays he holds down a job and can work a computer so I think he escaped unscathed. I never pushed him on anything steeper than a gentle slope after that though, I had learned my lesson. My mother never noticed the dented pram either, by the time it was no longer needed she had crashed it into the door frame so many times it looked like she had taken it banger racing.

After all this excitement, it was a bit of a relief when September rolled around and it was time to start school again as a junior. This time Melanie was in my class so we could sit together in some lessons. It felt a bit strange at first, moving to a different classroom every time we had a different lesson and it was hard to keep track of all the teachers' names. We were back to being the youngest in the school again and the kids in the top classes seemed really old. Some of them were thirteen and they were a lot bigger than us, we all did our best to stay out of their way.

We had only been back at school a few weeks and were just finding our feet when the whole class suddenly found themselves caught up in a sex scandal.

We didn't realise that at the time though as we were all still as clueless as each other.

It started with David Townsend. Every class has a David Townsend, the scruffy smelly one from the dirty family that everyone avoided. Our David was really smelly, I don't think he ever had a bath and his clothes were all filthy, when we did P.E. in our knickers and vests his were grey instead of white. His underpants always had holes in them and when he tried to climb the ropes even the teacher would look away to avoid having to look at the skid marks down the back of them. I felt quite sorry for him sometimes but wild horses wouldn't have dragged that out of me.

One morning David came into school with an envelope full of photographs. He told one of the boys that he had stolen them from his dad's bedroom and that they were dirty pictures. Now that wasn't surprising at all, we all expected that anything that came from David's house would be dirty. Anyway, the word started to get around the class and we started queuing up for a look. The photos were all black and white and were very confusing, we couldn't really make out what we were supposed to be looking at but Stephen Blackwell pointed out one that we all thought was a baby's bum.

We all knew David was weird, now we knew why, obviously, his parents were nuts. For a while we all sniggered about his dad having photos of bums and then went back to our own business and forgot all about David's pictures. By this time David had told so many kids about his collection that one of our teachers had got wind of it and confiscated the photos.

The next thing we knew David was taken out of class and hauled off to see the headmaster. It turned out the pictures were pornographic photographs of his mother and father. And I thought my parents were odd.

There was a proper hoo-ha going on now, someone said he had heard that the police were coming to arrest David. He said he had heard this by standing outside the staffroom door, he also said there were sounds of hysterical laughter coming from the room. I think David's pictures were doing the rounds by now.

The next morning we were all half way through double maths when we spotted David's parents skulking through the school gates. Heads down they made their way to the headmaster's office. I would have loved to have been a fly on that wall, can you imagine the embarrassment they must have been feeling? Apparently, what we in our innocence had mistaken for a baby's bum had in fact been a highly personal bit of Mrs Townsend's lady area.

Oh the humiliation, they must have wanted to run away and never come back. Imagine knowing that every kid in class 1B had all had a bird's eye view of your bits, not to mention every teacher in the school and probably a few dinner ladies as well. It was a proper scandal.

Today we would all be given counselling, we would be taken into a special room to explain what we'd seen by playing with dolls. Not that any of us knew what we'd seen anyway. I don't think the police were ever called and David never seemed to realise what a performance he'd caused. The teachers kept an eye on him after that though. They were forever searching his satchel and asking if he'd brought in anything from home. Maybe they just wanted to liven things up again in the staff room.

One thing I was sure of, being in junior school was turning out to be quite an eye opener.

CHAPTER TWENTY-ONE

It's A Knock Out

After the scandal at school things were pretty quiet for a while, it seemed no time at all until we were heading for Christmas. I was hoping there wouldn't be any Christmas plays at this school. I had been publicly humiliated far too often at my old school, I didn't need any more humiliation. As it turned out I was in luck, one morning at registration our teacher Mrs Burrell, announced that there would be no Christmas play that year. I was just heaving a sigh of relief when she dropped the next bombshell, instead of a play there was to be a Carol concert to which all the parents were invited. Oh no, my mother wouldn't be able to help herself, she would start singing.

Up to now nobody had heard her warblings, the kitchen window concerts were to come later. If the other kids heard her trying to outdo the choir it would be curtains for me, all the weeks of fitting in would count for nothing and I would be back to square one. I would just have to keep her away.

Now we had settled into our new home she was starting to get back to her old ways. She was worse now though because she had a screaming infant to get on her nerves as well as me. Now we had indoor toilets she began using them to get away. Sometimes she would lock herself in the downstairs one and scream and shout every swear word she could think of. Now I was at big school I heard these words more often and understood them more, I was shocked at what a potty mouth my mother had. I couldn't imagine what Melanie's posh mother thought of all this filth coming through the walls. I had never even heard her raise her voice, not even when Melanie's dad was hurtling down the road in his three- wheeler with us all in the back heading for certain death. Once again, she was keeping things from my dad, a new loan man had popped up and she was forever hassling my Aunty Dolly for money. She had also started ordering things willy-nilly from catalogues never thinking about how she was going to pay for it all. She was out of control.

We were keeping secrets again and I was back to having to think carefully before I answered anything my dad asked me. I would look at him for thirty seconds or so before giving him a response, this would give me time to mentally check the list of do's and don'ts that I kept in my head. I think he must have thought I was a bit slow, or deaf.

As I said before my brother was a late developer, that was putting it nicely. He was coming up to eighteen months now and showing no signs of walking or talking. I wasn't sure if this was anything to do with the big pram cover up so I spent ages trying to encourage him to do something. At the same time, I was praying that his first words wouldn't be anything to do with attempted murder.

Over time I came to realise it wasn't anything to do with me, he was just unbelievably lazy. He had put on loads of weight, you would never have believed how tiny he had been at first. He would sit on cushions like a little Buddha, pointing at things he wanted and grunting. He had worked out that there was no point in walking or talking when this could get you what you needed. It drove my mother nuts, he would point and grunt so she would give him what she thought he wanted. He would shake his head and point again and she would get him something else. This could go on for ages, he always wanted something different. After a few more minutes of pointing and grunting she would lose it.

"Get off your fat arse and get it your bloody self." she would scream before disappearing back into the loo for a bit more cursing.

After a while I came to the conclusion that he was doing it on purpose just to wind her up. When he pointed and grunted at me or my dad he was always happy with the first thing we gave him. I suspected that even at his tender age he was finding ways to get his own back. I was certain of this when he acquired his first mode of transport, a baby walker. My mother had become sick of being at his beck and call and seeing as he had no interest in walking on his own she bunged him in this and told him if he wanted anything he could now get it himself. Very responsible advice for a one year old.

He got the hang of it quickly and became quite a good driver. He could nip round furniture and even manage to negotiate the garden path all without incident. However, whenever my mother wasn't looking he would suddenly forget how to drive and go crashing into her legs or whizz by a bit too close and crack her ankle bone. To give him credit he always made it look like an accident but he couldn't hide the look on his face as he set off again, this was when I first realised he could smirk.

All this was before he started getting taught his lessons as I had been. I supposed there was no fun in whacking someone's backside when they couldn't even feel it through the thickness of a towelling nappy and thick rubber pants. He was a late developer on the potty as well. My mother would sit him on it for hours, he would be there pointing and grunting for ages without so much as a trickle or a fart. In the end my mother would have to give in and put a clean nappy on him. The instant she got all his clothes back on his face would turn a familiar shade of puce and he would proceed to empty everything he had into the new nappy. My mother would go bonkers.

I became convinced he was doing this on purpose too, I'm sure he was livening up his boring little life by torturing my mother. I had to hand it to him, he was good at it.

One tea time in late November my mother asked me to run to the shops around the corner, my dad was due home any time and she had run out of beans. She told me to get a big tin of Cross and Blackwell's and to hurry up there and back, I grabbed my coat and set off. It was dark early being November and it was cold and raining. I set off running as fast as I could, I didn't want to be outside any longer than I had to be. I didn't bother to take my glasses off as I thought nobody would see me and the dark and I would be quick.

I was almost at the shops, running as fast as my legs would carry me when it happened. I skidded around the corner and then suddenly everything went black. The next thing I knew I was sitting in a puddle on the wet pavement with a strange man trying to lift me up.

Now what had I done, who was this man and should I scream for help?

My parents had always told me not to talk to strange men (especially after the West Side Story incident) but you couldn't really ignore someone who had you by the armpits in a dark street. Before I could decide what to do I realised he was talking to me.

"Are you ok, can you stand up, are you hurt?"

I wished he would slow down a bit, I couldn't answer him if he kept on firing questions at me. I managed to get to my feet and told him I thought I was ok, then I asked him what had happened. He said he was hurrying home from work and when he got to the corner I had come thundering around the corner and run slap bang into him. He said I had hit him with such force that I had knocked him over and knocked myself out, he had been slapping my face for the last minute or so. Charming, there was no need for violence.

I was still a bit wobbly so he said he would take me home and explain things to my mother (good luck with that). I told him where I lived then he took me by the arm and we set off to my house. He must have been feeling really guilty, I thought it was probably all his fault.

We arrived home and he knocked on the front door. You can imagine my mother's face when she opened the door to find a strange man holding me up on the doorstep. My glasses had been knocked off in the crash and he had put them back on for me. The only trouble was he had missed one ear so my glasses were all askew, it must have looked to my mother as if Eric Morecambe was on her doorstep.

He explained everything that had happened and told my mother he was very sorry and hoped I was alright. She said I would be fine and thanked him for bringing me home, she told him it was all my fault anyway as I was always falling over. The man said goodbye then he patted me on the head and started to walk away, he had only taken a few steps when my mother called out to him.

"Excuse me a minute, when you picked her up I don't suppose there was a tin of beans around was there?" That woman's maternal instinct knew no bounds.

Christmas was coming up fast now, we were all practicing our carol singing at school every day in preparation for this bloody concert. Letters had been sent home inviting all the parents to come and join in, I had only one hope now. Everyone had been asked to leave small children at home so as not to disrupt our festivities by crying or screaming (blimey how bad did they think we were?) My mother would have to stay at home with my brother and my dad would never dare to come on his own in case someone looked at him, I might be ok after all.

Just as I was starting to relax up popped my cousin Janice with an offer to babysit, I could have killed her. She was always popping in to spend time with my brother. God knows why, he wasn't particularly interesting and couldn't hold a conversation. She always came at meal times, she liked to feed him. He liked her as well and would eat all his tea up for her without any fuss, quite the opposite to when my mother fed him. All his meals consisted of baked beans, it's the only thing he would ever eat and he consumed loads of them. I think this was another of his little tricks, by eating beans for breakfast, dinner and tea he was making sure that his nappies had the greatest effect on my mother. He would sit in his high chair while Janice spooned the beans into his mouth with hardly a dribble, behaving like the perfect child. When my mother fed him he would knock the spoon out of her hand and then when she bent down to pick it up he would dump the entire contents of his plate onto his head. I would tut and pretend to be as disgusted as she was while under the table I would be crossing my legs so I didn't wee, it was so funny and never got boring.

So, it was confirmed, my parents would be at the carol concert and there was nothing I could do about it. It wasn't only the thought of my mother's singing that scared me, I was thinking of my glasses. Nobody at school knew I even wore glasses except Melanie, I shoved them in my satchel every morning and only put them back on again when I went home after school. It was the same when I was playing out, I took them off before anyone saw me. The only times I wore my horrible glasses were in the house around my mother.

What would she say if she saw me on the stage without them? She would probably stand up in front of everyone and shout at me to put them on in thus ending my school life forever. I needed to come up with a plan here. Me and Melanie put our heads together and tried to find me a way out.

In the end, we decided that I would leave home wearing the glasses as usual, then take them off around the corner also as usual. I would stay well out of the way of my parents when they arrived to take their seats so that the first time they saw me without my specs would be on the stage. With a bit of luck my mother would be so busy trying to find a way of getting her singing noticed that she might not even notice. Even if my dad noticed he wouldn't say anything, I suspected he already knew I wasn't wearing them most of the time.

Afterwards if she asked about them I would say that I had taken them off to brush my hair when we were all getting ready and left them in the classroom by mistake. There hadn't been time to go back for them and I wouldn't need them anyway because there was nothing I had to read, we all knew the songs off my heart. With a bit of luck, I would get away with it.

At last the big night came. Everything was going to plan up to now, as soon as the audience started to file into the hall I got well out of the way. Melanie was peeping through the curtain and she told me when my parents came in and where they were sitting. Damn they were quite near the front, I had been hoping they would be at the back preferably behind some tall people with big heads. Still, there was nothing more to be done now, it was in the lap of the gods.
I couldn't even duck down behind the person in front of me because we were arranged in stages so everyone could get a look in, I was completely exposed so to speak.

Our year was on first, we were supposed to do three songs and then go and sit on the floor while the other years performed their songs. At the end, we would all get up for the big finale and ask the audience to join in. I knew my mother wouldn't be able to wait that long, she would be singing along before the first chorus in the first song. We took our places on the stage and waited for the curtain to open, this was it there was no turning back now.

The curtains opened, Mrs Wilding struck up the piano and we launched straight into Silent Night. Straight away I noticed my mother, I was trying not to look at her but I knew immediately that she'd sussed me She was nudging my dad and nodding her head towards me, I was terrified of what she would do next. I began to pray.

"Please don't let her stand up. Please don't let her stand up."

She didn't stand up, what she did next was nearly as bad though. She started mouthing to me in big exaggerated movements, dragging out the words in slow motion

"W H E.R E - A R E - Y O U R - G L A S S E S?"

"Oh no please stop, please don't do this now" I thought.

I tried to avoid looking at her but she was determined to catch my eye and to my horror put her hands to her eyes and started performing a terrible mime of someone wearing glasses. I could see her peering at me through the circles she'd made with her thumbs and forefingers. I could feel my face burning and completely forgot what I was supposed to be singing, I just stood there opening and closing my mouth like a goldfish. I desperately tried not to look at her and did my best to carry on.

Out of the corner of my eye I could see my dad trying to pull her hands down, his face looked redder than mine felt. She was slapping his hands away and pointing to her eyes, trying to get through to him about my missing specs, it was like some demented version of 'Give Us a Clue'. Why couldn't she just wait until afterwards and then ask me where my specs were, like a normal mother.

Somehow, I managed to make it through the three songs then went to sit with the rest of my class on the floor. My mother was behind me now but nothing on earth would make me turn around and look at her. By the end of the first song my dad finally managed to get her under control and behave like a sane person, I was just hoping none of my friends had seen her little performance.

When every year had done their bit we all stood up and crowded together then launched into the big finale 'We Wish You a Merry Christmas'. Yep I knew it, I could hear my mother's familiar tones above the rest of the audience, she was doing her best Julie Andrews.

Luckily none of the kids realised it was my mother singing because a few of our teachers had the same musical ambitions as she did and were all busy trying to outdo each other. God knows what it sounded like from outside.

When it was all over and everyone was leaving, my mother collared me about the glasses, I went into my well-rehearsed speech and she seemed satisfied. I told her I would come home with Melanie and her parents after I'd been to get my coat and things from the classroom. She said she would see me at home. Phew, I'd got away with it, mightily relieved I ran off to get my stuff.

When I arrived back home everything seemed normal, my brother was in bed and Janice was getting ready to go home. I was going to have some crackers and cheese for my supper and then go to bed, happy to have this day over with. My mother made some tea and we all sat down in front of the telly. I was just biting into my first cracker when my mother piped up,

"You are wearing your glasses at school, aren't you?"

Bum flaps, I'd been rumbled. I managed to splutter through my crackers that yes of course I was, how else would I see the blackboard? She seemed to believe me but I knew that the seeds of doubt were already planted in her brain. This wasn't over.

CHAPTER TWENTY-TWO

Green Stew and Deceit

Christmas came and went and the glasses thing didn't get mentioned again, I started to think I had really got away with the whole thing. Come to think of it I had been getting away with a lot lately. My hair was now long enough to put in bunches and I wore bobbles like the other girls, my mother had also stopped dictating what I wore. Admittedly I had been given some hideous clothes for Christmas but this time it was my dad's fault, he had been shopping himself and bought what he thought was the perfect attire for a young lady.

He had come up with a bright orange jumper with a shocking pink love heart stitched on the front of it, a pink blouse with puffy sleeves and a bright red skirt that stuck out like a big letter A. To finish the whole ensemble, he had bought me some shoes, big blocky lace up things with massively wide toes. From a distance, they looked dark in colour but when the light hit them you could see green, yellow and red tones. I had never seen anything like them before and have never seen anything like them since. You can imagine how thrilled I was on Christmas morning. My dad seemed really pleased though so I didn't have the heart to upset him, I said thank you and then hid them in the back of my wardrobe.

Now normally my mother would have taken great delight in forcing me to wear this outfit in public but up to now she hadn't even mentioned it. I could only think that I had my brother to thank for this reprieve, she was so busy running around in circles after him all the time that she had no energy left to torment me. Anyway, I was quite enjoying being a normal person for a change.

Soon it was January and time to go back to school. I got ready for my first day back, grabbed my satchel and when I heard Melanie knock on the door for me I was off. Just as we were nearly at the corner my mother shouted me back, she was holding out an envelope, what was she up to now? She passed the envelope to me and I saw it had my teacher's name on the front.

"Give that to Mrs Burrell" she said.

"What is it?" I asked, my heart was already sinking into my boots (not the multi coloured ones).

"It's just something I need to tell her" she said. "It's nothing you have to worry about."

Had she even met me? I could worry for England, I had been doing just that for as long as I could remember. I looked more closely at the envelope and saw she had sealed it up.

"Make sure she gets it" she said before going in and shutting the door behind her. Oh god something was going on here, whatever it was I knew it wouldn't end well for me.

Me and Melanie began slowly walking up the street.

"What do you think it is?" she asked me.

"No idea." I said "But it won't be good."

"Open it" she said.

How could I open it? She'd sealed it up, Mrs Burrell would know I'd looked. Melanie pointed out that Mrs Burrell wouldn't know there had been an envelope if I just gave her the note. After all, how many kids took notes to school in sealed envelopes?

She was right, she was a lot brighter than my old friend Denise.

Melanie peeked around the corner to make sure my mother was really gone then stood over me while I ripped open the envelope. I took out the note that was folded up inside, when I read what my mother had written I didn't know whether to laugh or cry.

Dear Mrs Burrell
Would you please make sure my daughter is wearing her glasses at all times. She is only allowed to take them off for P.E. lessons.
Thankyou

She had signed her name at the bottom and then underneath that she had added a bit more.

p.s
I am putting this note in a sealed envelope. If it has been opened please let me know and I will deal with it.

Ooh the crafty cow. Now what was I going to do, how was I going to get out of this one? Melanie was panicking more than me and it wasn't even anything to do with her, I don't know what she had done for excitement before I came along. There was only one thing for it, I tore the whole thing up and put it in my pocket, I would drop it in the litter bin outside school.

Out of sight out of mind.

I was on edge all morning at school, every time the classroom door opened I expected to see the headmaster with my mother behind him. I was glad when dinner time came around and I could go home and start the lying.

I sauntered into the kitchen hoping I looked like I hadn't a care in the world.

"Hello, what's for dinner?" I asked cheerfully.

I was giving my mother my best happy face, she should have seen straight through me immediately, I was never this cheerful around her.

"Beans" she said.

What a surprise, it was always beans, I got beans every dinner time. Just because my brother lived on them so did I, she wasn't cooking two different meals she said. Cooking? That was a laugh, all she did was open tins and warm them up. For some strange reason, she always put a spoonful of lard in with the beans while they were on the stove, she had been doing this all my life. I never met anyone who wasn't horrified by this and I never found out why she did it. It did explain why my brother was so fat though.

She was watching me closely while I sat at the table, I knew I had to tread carefully here and not overdo it. Me and Melanie had both agreed I should keep things simple so I didn't trip myself up.

"Did you give your teacher the note?" she asked, as she passed me my plate of lardy beans.

"Yes, I gave it to her before we did the register." I said.

"What did she say?" she asked.

"She just said thank you" I answered while trying to shovel beans into my mouth and avoid any more conversation.

She knew something was up, I could tell. Luckily my brother chose that moment to start turning purple and straining so I was saved for the time being.

It worked. My mother immediately forgot about me.

"You dirty little bugger." she screamed at him

"You've been sat on that bloody pot for an hour and now you decide you need a shit."

What a peach she was. I caught his eye, I swear he was winking.

Next morning as me and Melanie set off again my mother grabbed me at the door and handed me another envelope with Mrs Burrell's name on it, once again it was sealed. What the hell was she up to now, was she after a pen pal or what?

This time me and Melanie didn't even discuss it, once out of sight I ripped the envelope open and took out the note.

Dear Mrs Burrell

Yesterday I sent you a note asking you to make sure that my daughter wore her glasses at all times. I have a feeling she may not have given it to you. If you do not receive this one will you please let me know.

Thank you

I couldn't believe it, had she gone completely mad? If I wasn't giving the notes to Mrs Burrell how the hell could she let my mother know she wasn't receiving them. We had to think about it for a minute to make sure this wasn't some elaborate trap but no, she really was that dim. I could get out of this.

When dinner time came, I ran home for my beans and lard. As soon as I got in and took my coat off I put my plan into action.

"Mrs Burrell said I had to tell you that she got your notes and that I do wear my glasses all the time. Is that what you were writing to her about?" I said to my mother.

"Yes." she said "I had a feeling you weren't wearing them anymore, tell your teacher thanks for letting me know."

"I will." I told her.

After that I quickly changed the subject before she had time to stop and think about what she'd done. I could only think that having another baby when she was so old had done something to her brain. She was thirty five after all.

I carried on not wearing my glasses for another six months, still nobody at school except Melanie knew I even had any glasses. About a month before the summer holidays I got a scare though, we were all given letters to take home to say the school photographer would be coming round soon to take the end of term photos. My mother would expect to see me wearing my specs in mine, if I wasn't she was liable to come into school and have a go at my teacher for not making sure I was wearing them. That would lead to my subterfuge with the notes coming out, I would be in trouble until I was twenty-one.

What was I going to do?

I thought about keeping the specs in my pocket and shoving them on at the last second before the camera clicked. Maybe my classmates wouldn't notice and even if they did I could pretend I was playing a joke on my parents. No, that would be too risky, once they'd had a glimpse of Dame Edna they would never forget it. I figured I would just have to be taken really ill that day and stay at home, that was the only thing for it. I didn't even want my photo taking anyway.

As it turned out I was worrying for nothing, a couple of days later a card came in the post informing my mother that I was due for my yearly eye test. She made the appointment for after school and we went to the same shop that had been ruining my life for the last three and a half years.

While I waited for my turn I wondered what monstrosities my mother would pick for me this time. Elton John was just becoming popular, I could already hear my mother telling me how much I looked like him in my giant specs. Well it wouldn't matter what she picked anyway because I wouldn't be wearing them.

It turned out this was my lucky day, the optician told me my lazy eye was much better and I didn't need my glasses anymore and I should only put them on if I got a headache. I said I would but I was lying, even a brain tumour wouldn't make me wear them. He said there was no need to pick new ones and I could go home. Oh Joy, things were finally going my way.

One of the first people I told when I got back was Janice, she was going through the teenage spot phase at the time and was very angry about it. She said in a few years' time I would be glad of my massive specs because they would hide the massive spots that were in store for me. It was nice that she was so pleased for me.

To celebrate my new found freedom from my specs, I decided that for the first time in my life I would stay school dinners. I had always gone home for dinner before but I thought I should try everything once. My mother wasn't very impressed when I asked for the money but gave in grudgingly, she would be saving on beans. The next day I paid my money and looked forward to dinner time, wondering what delights would be served up. I hoped it wouldn't be beans.

Dinner time came and I got in line with the others in the dinner queue. I stood waiting for my turn, holding a big white plate, I felt like I was in Oliver Twist. The word came down the line that it was stew today. That was good, I liked stew, it was my dad's favourite and we had it all the time.

It got to my turn, I held my plate out to the dinner lady and she ladled a big dollop of stew onto my plate.

When I saw it I was puzzled, it was brown I had never seen brown stew before, ours was always green. I took it to the table anyway and sat down, I looked around the table but nobody else seemed to think their stew was strange. I nudged the kid next to me.

"Is the stew always this colour?" He looked at me like I was mad.

"Course it is, what colour did you expect?"

"Green." I said.

The whole table fell about laughing, they wanted to know who the hell has green stew and how do you even get green stew. How was I supposed to know? I didn't make the stuff, my mother did, I suppose that explained it all really. I tried it anyway and found it was really nice, the only thing was the strange little bits in it, I'd never seen anything like that in my mother's stew. I hated to ask but I had to know so I nudged the kid next to me again.

"What are these bits?" I got the same look again.

"Onions, what did you think they were?"

I shrugged and got on with eating my dinner. This was the first time I had ever eaten onions, my mother thought they were too spicy and exotic so we never had them. She had taken the term 'plain cooking' to a whole new level.

This was turning out to be a completely new learning experience for me. I finished my stew and lined up with the other kids to wait for pudding, I was delighted to find I'd picked sponge and custard day. I got to the front and was handed my bowl. Oh dear god now what? The custard was bright pink, I had only ever seen yellow custard. I'd come across pink blancmange and pink Angel Delight but never pink custard. If we were in April I would think this was an elaborate April Fool's joke.

Again, everyone was tucking in like this was all perfectly normal, there was no way I was asking about the food again so I just got on and ate it. It was delicious, the custard tasted like.... custard, apparently, the colour didn't make any difference to the taste.

I couldn't wait to get home and tell my mother about this, she would be amazed.

She wasn't. She just said it served me right for wanting to try school dinners and God knows what muck I'd been eating. I wanted to tell her it was better tasting muck than hers, but I didn't.

When my dad came home that night we sat around the table and he asked as usual what I'd been up to.

"I stayed school dinners." I announced proudly.

"Oh, that's good, what did you have?" he asked.

"Brown stew and pink custard." I told him.

He immediately asked if I was sure about not having to wear glasses anymore.

Later on, while my mother was washing up and trying to dodge my brother in his baby walker I asked my dad if he had ever come across brown stew. He said he could remember my Nanna's stew being brown. When I told him I'd had onions and liked them he was impressed, I was developing quite a cultured palate. I asked him why we never had onions.

"Your mother says we don't like them." He answered shaking his head sadly.

I never realised before that in his own way he suffered just as much as I did.

The next time my mother made stew I watched closely to see what she was doing, I soon got an explanation for why it was green. After putting in the meat and chopped up potatoes and carrots she added two whole tins of peas without draining them first. The strange colour in the stew was pea juice.

We weren't eating stew at all, we were eating thick pea soup. Not for the first time I wondered why my family was so different.

CHAPTER TWENTY THREE

Please Don't Pick Me, I'm The Third Degree

Junior school was whizzing by. There were so many different classes to go to and different things going on that the days seemed to go a lot faster than they had at primary school.

My mother was leaving my appearance alone more and more. My hair had never been this long and I was glasses free as well, from the outside I looked almost normal. I wasn't sure why my mother had stopped interfering with my appearance so much but maybe she was a bit more wary of me now I was getting older. After all I had a lot of dirt on her, maybe she was worried I would spill a few beans. I don't mean real ones, that was still my brother's job.

I had suffered a bit of an episode a few months before. One of my mother's many nieces was getting married and for the first and only time I was asked to be a bridesmaid. There were three of us, me, one of my cousins who was a year or two older than me and another one about six. I must say I was quite excited at the prospect.

On the morning of the wedding we were all taken to a proper hairdressers and given proper hairdos. My hair ended up in a massive beehive almost a foot tall, it was a real feat of engineering and made me look a bit like the cake. I wasn't on my own though so I didn't really mind, it was only for one day and nobody from school would be anywhere around to see me.

The wedding went smoothly, the sun was shining and everyone was happy. We posed for lots of photos and when we saw them later me and the other two bridesmaids looked like the Three Degrees. All in all, it wasn't a bad day. Until later.

After I arrived home I got out the hairbrush to put my hair back to normal but was stopped short by my mother yelling in my ear.

"Leave it, leave it."

Why was she talking to me like a dog? It turned out I wasn't allowed to touch my beehive, she thought it looked so nice and it had cost so much that I had to keep it in long enough to get my money's worth. I pointed out that it wasn't us that had paid for it, that was the bride's treat but she wouldn't listen. No matter, I figured after I had slept on it all night it would be such a mess she would tell me to wash it and get back to normal.

No such luck, the next morning it hadn't budged an inch, it was like a crash helmet. There must have been a gallon of hairspray still in it and it looked ridiculous when I was wearing my normal clothes. It was Sunday so I only had that day to get rid of it or I would have to take it to school the next day, I was in a panic.

I had to go to Aunty Dolly's that day for Sunday tea and looks on everyone's faces when I walked in was priceless. Malcom spent a good half an hour throwing things at my head, he said he was trying to knock my wig off. For once I encouraged him but even he couldn't put a dent in it, it was bomb proof.

After tea I was thrown a lifeline when it started raining. Yippee! I could walk home really slowly in the rain until my hair got soaking wet and that would do it. All the hairspray would be washed out and the whole structure would collapse. I set off at a snail's pace and took ages to walk home, I weaved in and out of avenues instead of going straight, I even doubled back a few times. At least nobody saw me as no one else was daft enough to be walking through the pouring rain.

It was only a ten-minute walk but it took me a good half an hour, I was soaked. I arrived home dripping wet, took my coat off and looked in the mirror. I couldn't believe it, my hair was untouched, it must have been waterproof as well. I began to think the stupid hairdresser had used liquid cement instead of hairspray.

Next morning it was still there, the only difference was it was leaning slightly to the left. Now I looked like a wonky wedding cake, or maybe the Leaning Tower of Pizza. With a sinking heart, I put my uniform on and looked in the mirror, I looked like a drag queen from St Trinian's.

Melanie bless her tried to be supportive but we both knew there was nothing for it but to face the music so off we went to school. As soon as the other kids saw me they went into hysterics. There was much poking and prodding and for the first lesson I had to endure various things bouncing off my head as they all took turns trying to dislodge it.

After playtime, I was called to the headmaster's office, I had never been in here before and I was scared stiff. I waited outside until I was called in. The headmaster, Mr Drury said he could appreciate how much time and effort had obviously gone into my hair but that it wasn't suitable for school and I would have to take it down. Oh thank God. I asked him if I could have a note to tell my mother this and he scribbled one off for me.

I couldn't wait to tell my mother and I ran home at dinner time and gave her the note, she was proper put out but she daren't argue with authority. Because it would be such a big job she said it would have to wait until tonight to wash it all out so I was forced to spend the afternoon with the offending tower on my head. It wasn't so bad now though, because the school had ordered me to remove it I was seen as something of a rebel. For the first time in my life I had a bit of street cred.

That night it took hours to get all the lacquer and backcombing out, my mother got in quite a tizzy with herself and things got quite painful. She was a bit surprised too when she came across two jelly tots and a pencil sharpener.

Everyone at school quickly forgot about my hair and things got back to normal. My favourite subjects at school were English and History and I was good at them, always coming top of the class when we had tests. I wasn't so good at the practical lessons like woodwork and art. The practical lessons were all done in a separate building away from the main part of the school. It was called the conversion unit (don't know why) and it was basically a giant greenhouse. It was built entirely of glass panels and was split into separate sections, cookery, art, needlework and wood and metalwork. There were no walls to separate us so you could see what everyone else was doing in their lessons.

I don't know who had come up with the idea of a glass building but it must have been someone who hated children. In the summer months it was torture. The temperature inside would soar and we would all slowly roast. Imagine a hundred and forty kids crammed into this glass case in the middle of June. It would have been bad enough anyway but add to that the ten or so ovens going in the cookery section and the kiln roaring away in the art department and it was hell on earth.

We weren't allowed drinks in there so we would quickly start to dehydrate, after half an hour or so we would all be delirious. The last thing you needed in a place that contained tools, needles, knives and other sharp objects was for all the kids to be staggering around off their heads. It was dangerous to say the least.

Whatever lesson you were in it was impossible to stay awake, slowly your eyes would droop and your head would get lower and lower until you zonked out on the desk. This could be very alarming for the kids operating sewing machines, if your head fell onto the machine while your foot was still on the pedal it could get nasty. And it would do you no good to shout for the teacher to dislodge your nose from the needle because she would be passed out too. It was madness.

One summer we got a new art teacher and for the first time the kids doing their art lessons got a reprieve from the sauna. This new teacher was quite horrified when she felt how hot it was in there so she used to make everyone do their lesson outside in the sunshine. It was great, we would all be stretched out on the grass, sketching and doodling while topping up our tans.

Meanwhile, if you peeped through the steamed up windows you could see everyone else stewing and suffering. There would be roughly a hundred little bodies draped over various tables, sewing machines and chopping boards. It looked like Jonestown after everybody had drunk the Kool Aid.

One day after half term we turned up for our English lesson to find out we had a new teacher. His name was Mr Webster, he was skinny with wild ginger hair and a beard and he wore glasses so thick that his eyes looked like pinholes. He was here to teach us English and drama and he was extremely passionate about it. Our usual drama lessons had consisted of standing in the hall, half-heartedly waving our arms around pretending to be trees. After a couple of weeks with Mr Webster we were putting on plays that wouldn't have looked out of place in the National Theatre. Nothing like them had ever been seen before at our school

One of the older classes were performing Perseus in the Underworld complete with gorgons, dead people and everything. All the classes in the school were taken into the assembly hall to watch the first performance. One big lad called Melvin was playing the part of a king who gets murdered, we all watched enthralled as the dramatic music boomed out of the speakers. Suddenly Melvin was stabbed in the stomach by someone with a sword, we all gasped in horror as blood splattered all over the floor. Then he spun round clutching his stomach with bloody hands and spewed a pint of blood out of his mouth onto the floor directly in front of the first row. It was all too much. Everyone was shocked, not knowing if something had gone terribly wrong and Melvin had been murdered for real. One poor girl sitting at the front fainted dead away and had to be carried out.

After the performance ended and after a few letters of apology had been sent out to parents Mr Webster was told to tone it down a bit. Most of us weren't allowed to watch horror films on the telly, even Frankenstein in black and white. So to see a realistic disembowelling inches from our noses was a bit disturbing.

Mr Webster wasn't happy at all about having to compromise his artistic integrity and ranted about it for weeks. He still managed to make a statement in everything he did though. Our usual Easter offering where we dressed up as eggs and chicks and pranced around was transformed into a biblical epic that saw poor Jimmy Parker hoisted ten foot into the air on a giant cross while wearing a nappy.

One day in Mr Webster's class the worst possible thing happened to me, I was noticed.
I had always followed my dad's teachings. Blend into the background and hope nobody notices you're there at all. It hadn't always been easy with my mother being how she was but I thought I was managing ok.

This day we were told to go off and write a poem, Mr Webster said it could be about anything we wanted so off I went and wrote one. I had always found it easy to make up daft rhymes and verses so I rattled this one off in half an hour. It was something about thinking there was a ghost following me and then finding out it was a leaf stuck to my shoe.

It was pretty basic, I even rhymed ghost with toast he only bit I recall now is:

I could be at home eating hot buttered toast,

Instead of out here with what could be a ghost.

It was hardly award winning poetry but was enough to impress Mr Webster. He grabbed me after the lesson demanding to know how I had come up with that in half an hour. He said it wasn't just the words, apparently, my timing was brilliant too, oh no I didn't like where this was going. Then he said he was so impressed he was going to enter my poem in a competition. I was horrified but said ok, anything to get away.

I didn't win anything but it didn't matter, I had been brought to his attention now. Before this happened, he had a few favourites in the class that would always get a mention. If he was giving an example of something he would slip their name in to the conversation. One of these favourites was Jackie Benson, he would say something like:

"It could have been anyone your age, say Jackie Benson over there."

Jackie Benson would look smug while everyone else muttered 'teacher's pet' under their breath. One lesson I was staring out of the window, lost in thought when I suddenly heard my name. I looked up startled to see thirty odd pairs of eyes looking at me quizzically, and one pair belonging to Jackie Benson looking daggers. I had been used as one of Mr Webster's examples, oh please no, don't let this be happening.

It was too late, it had happened and the damage was done. After that he would use any excuse to bring my name into the conversation, it was excruciating. If he needed someone to come out and help with something he would make a big show of looking around at us all. I would be sitting there cringing.

"Please don't pick me. Please don't pick me."

He would pick me. Worse than that, the other kids had noticed and were starting to come out with comments. Being called a teacher's pet was bad enough but some of them started to call me Mrs Webster, it was horrible. Looking back, I can see that he was trying to do me a favour, he was trying to give me a bit of self-confidence. I didn't want any part of that, I was quite happy to be ignored and left alone

I was just glad I hadn't been spotted before the Easter play, that could have been me up there on that cross.

CHAPTER TWENTY-FOUR

What's That Smell?

The summer holidays had come around once again and we were about half way through the six weeks. Me and Melanie had been out most of the days playing and riding our bikes around and we were getting a bit bored. There was a new craze going around that year, anyone who was any one had to possess the newest thing or you just weren't cool.

The thing in question was a pair of 'Clackers' which were a pair of rock hard heavy, plastic balls (about as big as ping pong balls) suspended on two strings with a small plastic handle thing in the middle. The idea was to get the balls to bang together, firstly above your arm and then below it. Once you'd got them to bang together you moved your wrist up and down faster and faster to get the balls to make a clacking sound. Clackers, get it? They made a proper racket, the streets were ringing with the sound of balls banging together (pardon the expression) for months as every kid in the district competed to see who could make their clackers clack for the longest. The only trouble was if you lost the rhythm, then the balls would come crashing down at full speed onto your forearm and it hurt like hell.

We were all black and blue all the time, we compared bruises like war wounds. Sometimes your bruises were so bad that "clacking" became impossible and until you had healed up a bit you had to give it up. As soon as the bruises faded you would be back at it until you smashed your arm to bits again and you had to have another week off.

After a while someone realised that all the kids in Britain were walking round with fractures and Clackers were removed from the market completely. A while later a safer version of them came out with much lighter, softer balls but they were no fun so they quickly went away again.

As I said we were getting bored that summer and one day we had a bit of a brainwave. We decided to make our own house in the front shed. Our new house had a shed in the back garden and another one opposite the front door, the back one had a window but the front one didn't. My dad kept all his gardening stuff in the back one so we weren't allowed to play in there, but all we kept in the front one were mine and my dad's bikes so he said we could have that to play in.

We turned into a proper palace, well the sort of palace with no windows and a concrete block in the corner that housed the dustbin. We scavenged everything we could and by the end of the first day we had a rug on the floor, a couple of chairs, a picnic table, some cushions and even some art work on the walls (my painting by numbers picture of a ballerina). We had our own key so we could lock the door, although the first time we locked it we realised we needed some sort of illumination or we were sitting in the pitch black. I tried to light a few candles for ambience but my mother had a fit and called me a bloody arsonist so I borrowed my dad's torch instead.

On our first night (well just after tea) in our new home we decided to throw a bit of a housewarming party. We invited Susan as she was family and she brought her friend Jane who arrived with her younger sister Mary. For entertainment we had a selection of board games and for nibbles we had a packet of Ritz crackers that I had nicked from the kitchen cupboard.

We didn't need music as we had my mother screeching a melody or two through the open kitchen window, she sounded much better through a locked door. After a few games of Kerplunk we decided we would have a fiddle with my Ouija board. My mother didn't know that I still had this, she had taken it away from me the year before when I scared myself silly talking to invisible people. I refused to go to bed without all the lights on for a week after my mother sent them away.

Jane and Mary were not that keen to play, they were very religious and went to church all the time as well as Sunday School every Sunday (obviously). I had only been to Sunday School once when I was six. My parents forgot to pick me up and I had to be taken home by the Salvation Army.

Anyway, it was my house so if they wanted to stay they had to join in, we set up the board and all put our fingers on the pointy thing. After a while it began to move around the board and soon we were talking to an old woman who said we should call her Granny. We thought were communicating with a nice old lady spirit here so we asked her a few things. Stuff like how old she was, how long had it been since she'd 'passed on' and was it nice where she was, all the kinds of things you ask a dead person. When we'd finished quizzing her we asked if she had a message for any of us.

She said yes she did and it was for the three young ones which meant me, Melanie and Mary. We waited excitedly to see what our message was, it wasn't what we were expecting. Sweet old 'Granny' told us she was going to come and see us that night when we'd gone to bed and pull our legs off. We looked at each other in complete horror, Mary took her finger away and started crying. Then Granny spelt out the words that she was going to give us a sign. Within a couple of seconds there was a loud knocking from underneath the picnic table.

We went mental, we all scrambled for the door at once, knocking over Granny's board as well as all the nibbles, chairs and my dad's bike which was still in there covered up by a flowered tablecloth. We were screaming and crying and practically killing each other to get through the door first. Just as Melanie was reaching for the key to unlock it the torch went out and we were plunged into complete blackness. Our terror knew no bounds then. In the darkness Melanie couldn't see the key any more so started pounding on the door with her bare fists, I was trying to drag her out of the way so I could feel for the key. Meanwhile Mary started screaming hysterically that something had got her leg and was pulling on it.

That did it, the thought that Granny was in there with us gave me some kind of inner strength and I found the key in the lock. I turned it and we all fell out into the daylight in a big sobbing, screaming, snotty mess, straight into my mother who was on her way to find out what the bloody hell was going on.

When we stopped hyperventilating and explained about Granny trying to pull Mary's legs off she went nuts. She stormed into the shed, picked up the Ouija board and threw it into the dustbin telling me to get in that bloody house now before she threw me in the sodding dustbin after it. She was ever so sympathetic.

Everyone was sent home, the shed was locked up and my mother kept the key. I had a feeling we'd been evicted already.

That night I was terrified to go to bed. My mother told me not to be stupid, nothing was going to touch my legs, we'd just got ourselves into hysterics. She wouldn't let me keep the light on so the only light coming into my room was from the lamppost at the end of our block.

Luckily I had Melanie to talk to. For Christmas I had been given a pair of telephones, you could connect them together with a long wire and talk to someone in another room. Me and Melanie had slung the wire out of my bedroom window into hers and we had a phone each. We weren't supposed to talk on them when we were in bed but we both needed morale support that night while we tried to keep our legs in place until the morning.

Our whispered conversation that night consisted mainly of,

"Are you still awake?"

"What was that noise?"

"Can you hear that?"

Every little sound sent us crying under the blankets. I was praying for morning, swearing that never again would I try and talk to dead people. After an hour or so I think Melanie must have either fallen asleep or bled to death when Granny showed up and pulled her legs off. I couldn't get her to answer me. I hung up the phone at my end and tried to sleep.

At about one o clock in the morning my phone started buzzing, I snatched it up quickly in case it woke my mother. I already had one mad old bloodthirsty biddy to worry about, I didn't need another. It was Melanie and she sounded giddy with relief. She said Susan had just come into her room to confess, she said she felt too guilty to sleep. She told her that we had been set up and her and Jane were in on it together. They had both been pushing the pointy thing around the board, Susan had done the knocking under the table and when we all went mental she switched the torch off. When poor Mary thought Granny had her legs it was really her sister Jane pulling at her ankles. They thought it was so funny at the time but now Susan felt bad.

The rotten pair of cow bags, I could have strangled the pair of them. Not only had they almost given me a heart attack, they had got me into trouble with my mother and to top it all off they had got me evicted from my shed.

The next morning I explained everything to my parents, how we had been taken advantage of by the two older bad girls who thought it was funny to scare little girls. I begged them to let us have the shed back and promised we'd be good and quiet and never talk to dead people ever again.

My mother was dead against it but my dad said we could have it back as long as he didn't hear any more about us getting into trouble. He gave me the key and we moved back in.

After that we were very choosy who we let in, Susan was on probation and Jane never came around anymore, I think she was too busy visiting Mary in the mental hospital.

We played nicely, like good girls for at least a week before we got into bother again. It was a Saturday morning and we had got bored watching Multi Coloured Swap Shop with Noel Edmonds (he wasn't actually watching it with us, he was in it). Besides, what good was a multi coloured swap shop if your telly was still black and white? We went out to play in the shed for a bit, taking some games and books with us. We were just unlocking the door when a big black and white cat came wandering up to us, it was really friendly and followed us inside.

After an hour of being stroked and cuddled, it curled up on one of our cushions and went to sleep. We had another brainwave then. We decided what every home needed was a pet, we would keep the cat in our shed, nobody would know it was there. We could feed it with stuff we could pinch from our mothers and I could let it out in a morning when I got up and then again after school.

We were very excited, we called our new pet Dorothy (we both loved the Wizard of Oz) and I tied a big pink ribbon round her neck from my dolls clothes box. While my mother was busy fetching things that my brother was pointing at I sneaked into the kitchen to see what I could find. I liberated a tin of pilchards and some meat paste and took it back to the shed. Meanwhile, Melanie had sneaked a bottle of milk from her kitchen.

Dorothy was very happy when she woke from her nap to find a banquet waiting for her. She gobbled half the tin of pilchards, a big dish of milk and then we spread a bit of meat paste onto a Ritz cracker that was left over from the séance and she ate that too. We played with her for a bit longer then she curled up on her cushion and went back to sleep again. We decided to go out and play for a bit and let Dorothy sleep it off, we would let her out when we came back. We locked the door and went off to play, taking the key with us to keep out trespassers.

We didn't mean to stay away so long but we got a bit carried away and lost track of time. We discovered that a little fun fair had been set up in one of the fields nearby and everyone from school was there. I had my pocket money on me and Melanie had a few coins so we had a good look around and had a few rides on the swing chairs and the merry go round. We stuffed ourselves sick with candyfloss and drank cans of coke. You could get a lot for your money in the seventies.

Eventually we remembered Dorothy still locked in the shed, she would probably need to be let out now after that big meal. We set off for home in a hurry. We got back to our street and were just about to turn the corner to our houses when we heard an awful wailing noise. My first thought was that my mother was singing again. As we turned the corner we came face to face with both of our mothers as well as some other neighbours, they were all crowded around our shed.

They were trying an assortment of different keys into the lock on the shed door.

The wailing was a lot louder now, me and Melanie looked at each other in fear, we were well and truly in bother now. The wailing was obviously Dorothy, anxious to get out of her luxury prison. My mother grabbed hold of me none too gently.

"You'd better not have a bloody cat in there." she hissed.

What the hell did she think was making a noise like that, a rabbit?

"Give me that key NOW."

Several of the neighbours jumped back, she was getting herself into full combat mode now. I passed her the key and prepared to run but one look at her red face and the vein bulging in her forehead and I thought better of it. I would rather have witnesses for what might happen next.

My mother put the key in the lock, turned it and opened the shed door. I don't know what hit her first, the god-awful smell of cat pee mixed in with regurgitated pilchards and curdled milk or Dorothy as she flew out of the door at ninety miles an hour and hit my mother smack in the face before escaping over her shoulder.

It all got a bit loud after that, my mother was screaming blue murder and the neighbours were shouting at me and Melanie because they'd had to put up with the caterwauling all afternoon. Even Melanie's mother who never raised her voice or got into a tizzy was looking quite sternly at us. One lady who we didn't recognise was very angry with us, she was accusing us of kidnapping (cat-napping?) her cat. It turned out Dorothy was actually called Henry and lived around the corner with this woman, she had only let him out for a minute into the back garden and she was terrified he'd been run over. She had been wandering around looking for him when she heard him screaming for help.

That probably explained some of the smell, Henry/Dorothy had been spraying tom cat scent all over our things, either before or after he/she had thrown up everything we had fed the greedy bugger.

I was forced to apologise to everyone, for some reason I got all the blame because it was my shed. Henry's owner stormed off to find him as he'd run off again in all the commotion, I figured when she saw the pink bow around his neck I would be doing some more apologising. The key was taken away permanently and we were never allowed to play in the shed again. My mother said I couldn't be trusted.

We didn't really mind losing our den anyway. It was a good two years before the smell disappeared.

There were still two weeks to go before the new school term started and we were still bored. Since everything we did to entertain ourselves ended in disaster, Melanie's dad stepped up with an idea.

He worked on the geriatric ward at the hospital and he thought it would be a good idea to take us to work with him. He said we could make ourselves useful by helping out with the old people. We could make them cups of tea and read to them and stuff.

My parents thought this was a great idea, it would keep me out of trouble and out of my mother's way until she could pack me off to school again. So on the Monday morning we climbed into the back of his three wheeled car and sped off to entertain the old folk.

I don't know quite what I was expecting but it was very different from what actually greeted us when we arrived. I thought the place would be full of sweet old ladies with rosy cheeks smiling and offering us toffees, perfect grandma material. Maybe they would be in hospital with sprained ankles or the odd broken hip. We could push them around the gardens in their wheelchairs and they would be so grateful to us for giving up our holidays to help look after them.

What we actually got looked like night of the living dead. Everyone was propped up in a chair, pillows stuffed everywhere to stop them falling onto the floor.

They were all thin and yellow looking and most of them couldn't even speak, they made strange noises and laughed suddenly for no reason. It was terrifying. I had promised my parents I would never try and talk to dead people again and here I was making tea and biscuits for them. I think they were only in hospital because nobody wanted to look after them.

Melanie seemed quite shocked as well, her dad hadn't prepared her at all. To top it off he disappeared onto another ward as soon as we got there and left us to get on with it. The other nurses didn't seem to want us there at all and were very snotty, every time we asked them a question they were really bitchy. They gave us all the dirty jobs, instead of nursing we were cleaning. This wasn't at all what I'd had in mind, we were being used as slave labour. While we were doing all the work the nurses were sitting in the staff room, drinking coffee and gossiping.

I couldn't wait for Melanie's dad to finish his shift and take us home. I felt sure once I told my parents what it was really like they wouldn't want me to go back. This was no place for an innocent little schoolgirl.

Maybe it wasn't, but they thought it was the perfect place for me. They said it would give me backbone (I told them I already had one) and my mother said it would do me good to see that not everyone had a cushy life like me. Eh?

So, the next morning we were packed off again. At least for the rest of the week Melanie's dad was only working half days so we could come home at dinnertime. All that morning I watched the clock, willing it to go faster, I had made endless cups of tea that morning and nobody ever drunk them. Half an hour after I'd served everyone tea the nurses would tell me to clear their cups away. I would throw all the tea away, wash the cups, put the kettle back on and serve tea again, it was complete madness. The only time any nurses bothered with these poor people was if one of them fell out of their chair. Then two of them would come in, hoist the poor old dear back into the chair and bugger off again, they didn't seem to do much for their wages. Thankfully, after I'd served about fourteen rounds of tea and biscuits it was time to leave.

When I arrived home that afternoon there was great excitement in our house, my brother had finally spoken his first word. Unfortunately, the word was Pig. Now my dad hated this word, he didn't mind people calling him names (I told you he was easy going) as long as nobody called him a pig. I never found out why.

My mother had about five hours to break my brother of this new behaviour before my dad got home. He would want to know how my brother had picked up such a word and no doubt I would get the blame. Never mind that at least ten times a day my mother would scream.

"You dirty little pig."

"You greedy little pig."

"You lazy little pig."

It didn't take a pigging genius to work it out.

My brother was really proud of his new vocabulary. No more pointing and grunting, now it was pointing and 'Pig'.

Everything was 'Pig', a cup, a toy, his pram, my mother, all came under the same heading 'Pig'. I thought this was hilarious, I couldn't wait for my dad to get home. It would even be worth getting the blame just to see his face.

For the next few hours my mother tried everything she could think of to stop my brother. She tried slapping his hand every time he said it, she would scream into his ear, she tried being nice, giving him treats, no matter what she tried he was having none of it. He had found his voice and he was happy about it.

Six o clock came around and in came my dad. He said hello to me and my mother and then went into the living room where she was trying to hide my brother. We both held our breath and waited, I peeped round the door. My brother was in his baby walker in front of the telly and he turned round when he heard my dad come in. His face lit up with pride, he scooted over to my dad and stuck a pudgy finger in my dad's leg, then he beamed up at him and blurted out.

"Pig."

I couldn't help it I burst out laughing, my dad's face was a picture.

"What did he say?" he spluttered. My brother helped him out by repeating it.

"Pig." he laughed.

"Where the hell did he learn that?" my dad wanted to know.

I told him quickly it was nothing to do with me. I hadn't even been here when he found his voice, I'd been serving refreshments in the Twilight Zone. My mother came in with some excuse about his favourite story being the three little pigs but it wasn't convincing.

From then until he went to bed my brother practiced his new word non- stop. My dad was horrified and told my mother they couldn't take him out anywhere until he learnt some better words. He wouldn't be called a pig in public, especially by a two year old. It was so funny, my brother was grounded before he could even walk on his own.

Fortunately, in the next few weeks he learned a few more words. Unfortunately, they were, sod, bugger and damn. This was priceless, my mother was in hell, she never knew when he was going to come out with one of them. She couldn't stay in all the time, she had to go shopping and she had to take him with her.

She would stick him in his pushchair and fly round the supermarket in record time before he could show her up. She would be ok until someone decided to speak to the happy little chap in the pushchair, someone always had to come up to talk to him.

"Hello little man, are you shopping with your mammy?"

My brother would give them a winning smile and shout:

"Bugger" or one of his other little gems.

My mother would turn bright red and stutter an apology before running out of the shop like her arse was on fire. Our family would be getting a reputation for being rough, my parents worst nightmare. My brother was a juvenile delinquent.

He was also developing a real temper (can't think where he got that from) and he would take it out on my mother by screaming and throwing things at her. She would put him in another room until he calmed down and you could clearly hear him all over the house venting his frustration. I was sent in once to try and subdue him with a milky bar but he barely noticed me, he was rocking backwards and forwards, nutting his teddy bear and chanting at the top of his voice.

"Pig, Bugger, Sod, Damn."

It was beyond funny, why didn't someone invent camcorders sooner?

After the first two days working at the home for the terminally bewildered I really didn't want to go any more. I pleaded with my parents to tell Melanie's dad that I had a prior engagement but they were too wrapped up in the shame of having a foul mouthed toddler and told me to stop whining and get on with it.

So, with a heavy heart I set off again for my third day of tea making and floor mopping, little did I know it was to be my last ever. The first couple of hours were uneventful, I served up and threw away several dozen cups of tea, shouted good morning to a few of the poor zombies in their chairs and was just going off to find a mop when I noticed a poor old man trying to get my attention. He was beckoning me to come over to him, when I obliged he started grunting (I'd only just got rid of one grunter and here was another) and pulling at his pyjama bottoms.

At first I didn't know what he wanted, until I saw what he was trying to pull out of his pyjamas. Then I realised that he must want a wee. I shouted at him that I would go and fetch a nurse but he didn't seem to like this, he carried on fiddling with himself while the grunting got louder. Melanie came over to see what all the noise was about and this seemed to make his need for a wee even more urgent. The noise got louder.

One of the nurses was passing on her way for another cup of coffee and heard the commotion. She came in, took one look at the scene before her and tried to drag me and Melanie away while at the same time shouting at the poor old man to stop what he was doing right now. This was terrible, I tried to tell her that all he wanted was a wee but she wasn't listening. She had us by the elbows and was propelling us towards the doors. We were extremely confused by now, what kind of nurse would shout at you for needing a wee?

Don't forget we were very innocent in those days. Nobody had ever heard of the word 'paedophile' and if we couldn't even tell pornographic photos when they were under our nose, how were we supposed to know what this poor old man was really after.

Today's kids would be traumatised by the things that happened to us but we didn't even realise anything had happened, we were completely oblivious.

At least the dirty old bugger did us a favour. The nurse had a quiet word with Melanie's dad and on the way home he told us that we never had to go and serve tea there again. My parents were told that my services were no longer needed but not told why. Wouldn't you know it, my mother said that it was probably my fault.

As my brother would say:

"Bugger."

CHAPTER TWENTY-FIVE

End of the Road

I had been in junior school for more than three years now and I was twelve years old, almost a teenager. The last three years had gone by so fast, I was in my last year now and when we broke up for the summer holidays that would be it. In September I would be going to high school and I was dreading it, I had got used to my little school and didn't want to move to the new one. At my school all the kids came from around a few blocks of where I lived, at the new one there would be kids from all over the town, it was scary. I had been for a visit to have a look at the new school and it was enormous. It looked like a big factory, there were big separate buildings two and three storeys high. It looked terrifying and I knew I'd never find my way around it.

Still, that was in the future, I would worry about it when the time came. For now I was making the most of still being here. I was looking relatively normal now, my mother hadn't tried to cut my hair for the last three years and it was past my shoulders. It was the longest it had ever been, I had always dreamed of having long hair. So what did I do? I went off to the hairdressers on my own and had it cut off, that's what.

It was the era of Slade, The Sweet and Suzy Quatro and everyone wanted the same haircut that they had. It was called the Shaggy Dog and it really only suited people with the right kind of hair. Unfortunately, I didn't possess such hair, Melanie and Susan had the right hair, smooth, straight and shiny. Mine was none of the above, it had suddenly developed a life of its own. All those years of my mother sticking hairgrips into it willy nilly had finally paid off, the front bit had decided to develop a kink that no amount of brushing could ever sort out. The rest was a cross between wavy and frizzy and I hated it. All I wanted was straight smooth hair.

I had seen girls in films ironing their hair to straighten it, I would never be able to manage to do that on my own and there would be no point in asking my mother to help. She wouldn't even iron my dad's shirts because she said if she didn't wear them, why should she have to do it. The few times she'd attempted it she had left big scorch marks on them, imagine what she could do to my head.

I came out of the hairdressers feeling very modern, the Shaggy Dog called for the top part of your hair to be cut short, while the rest was left long and shaggy (get it). It was like two hairstyles in one and in later years would be renamed the Mullet. It wasn't my finest moment but at least I had done this by myself and not had it forced on me by my mother. Anyway, while the other girls resembled Suzi Quatro, I resembled a toy poodle. Luckily I was completely oblivious to this and for the first time ever I felt trendy.

My parents were not very impressed by my new look, my mother said I had ruined my hair and my dad just looked bemused. He was a bit overwhelmed by seventies fashions, most dads were, especially the ones with teenage sons. All of a sudden their little boys had long hair and were wearing high heels (platform shoes were coming into fashion) and it scared them silly.

A prime example of this was going on opposite my house. Mr Francis across the block was called Alan, he named his firstborn son Alan after himself and had always been extremely proud of him. In the last few months Alan Jnr, who was just seventeen had thrown himself wholeheartedly into everything seventies. He didn't just have the long hair and the clothes, he also wore glittery make up when he went out to the disco. His dad was completely dumbfounded, he had never heard 'glam rock' mentioned before and he was having none of it. That year the street rang with the sounds of Mr Francis bellowing:

"Get back in this house and stop making a show of us you bloody great puff."

It was very amusing for the rest of us, the neighbours who didn't have teenage sons could have a right good laugh.

Alan Jnr had got a job at my dad's factory and my dad said all the other blokes took the mickey out of him all day long about his dress sense and his hair (he stopped short of the make up for work). Alan Jnr didn't care my dad said. He would toss his long blonde hair over his shoulder and totter off in his platforms as if he was off to appear on Top of the Pops.

Me and Melanie would watch him coming home in the early hours of the morning sometimes from our bedroom windows. He always stayed out much later than his dad would allow so to avoid being rumbled he would shinny up the drainpipe and squeeze through his bedroom window. He used to bribe his little brother to leave it open for him. We would be crying with laughter watching him trying to climb the drainpipe in his high heels then disappearing headfirst through the window until just his platforms were visible.

Me and Melanie were in awe of him. He was the nearest thing to a pop star we had ever seen and we thought he was really cool. Unfortunately his dad didn't find him nearly as fascinating as we did, he spent all his time trying to stop people seeing him. I swear some days when he was screaming at him to get his fancy pants back in that house there were tears in his eyes.

My dad used to sympathise with Mr Francis but I think he was just thankful that my brother wasn't old enough to be a glam rocker. Alan Jnr moved out a couple of years later, I sometimes wondered if he embraced punk rock in the same way when that came around. I pictured him wearing bin liners and with safety pins through his nose and ears. I think that would probably have killed his poor father.

Mr Francis was just one of the many confused fathers around back then. They just couldn't understand why their previously sensible sons were now prancing around looking like their daughters.

They weren't just embarrassed, they were ashamed and bewildered. Someone should really have started a support group for them all, something like A.A. It could have been called M.A (Mortifieds Anonymous).

Around this time, we got some new next door neighbours, they were called Joan and Colin and they had four boys aged from two to eight. They were a bit loud but really nice and Joan was really funny. She loved to sing as well and she would turn her stereo up really loud and let rip, just like my mother. She was very much into Connie Francis, a singer from the fifties and played her albums all the time. You could hear it full blast through the walls in our house so my mother would join in, they would both be giving it loads, belting out all of Connie's ballads. It was like some mad female version of Robson and Jerome, they would compete to see who could hit the highest note and hold the longest note. My mother loved it, at last she had found someone else who didn't mind making a show of herself. I had a feeling the teatime concerts would be drawing a bigger audience under the kitchen window from now on.

A few months after Joan and Colin moved in there was a bit of a hoo-ha about them. Someone found out that (shock, horror) they weren't actually married and it was considered a proper scandal. The first I knew of it was when I heard Melanie's mother whispering to my mother that all of Joan's children were 'bastards.' I was shocked to the core to hear such language coming from such a posh lady, she never even said the words 'bloody' or 'hell'. What on earth could be going on?

I could only assume that she had been listening to my potty mouthed mother through the walls for so long that she had been infected. Joan's boys might have been a bit rough and ready but I wouldn't have said they were bastards, that was a bit strong. I didn't know that's what they called you if your parents weren't married, or as Melanie's mother put it 'Living in Sin'.

Anyway, it caused a bit of gossip for a few weeks until the lady opposite cleaned her back doorstep one day with no knickers on and they all moved on to pick on her. If Joan ever knew she was being talked about she never let on, I don't think she would have cared anyway. She and Colin got married a few years later when they eventually got around to it but by that time everyone was used to them so it made no difference anyway.

For all the friendliness between my mother and Joan my mother would never allow my brother to play with her boys. She said they were too rough and not the sort he should be mixing with. Not that she let him mix with anyone else, he was four years old now and confined to the back garden. He never went out anywhere unless he was with my parents or me.

I found this very strange, when I was not much older than him I had been out playing all day only coming in to be fed. I was off balancing on the top of a rusty old steam roller and running round the playground with all the other kids. Nobody checked up on me much and I was a girl, meanwhile the boy of the family was locked in the garden and watched like a hawk. It wasn't just me who found it strange, the neighbours did too, I heard one of them once call him 'the boy behind the fence' as if he had no name.

My mother wouldn't let him out of her sight. It was as if she had waited so long after my arrival for another child that now she'd got him she wasn't letting go. For all the mental breakdowns she had while he was small he really was the apple of her eye. He never appreciated how much she adored him and never really seemed to even like her that much. He was like me, he much preferred my dad as well.

I think the first couple of years with her might have traumatised him a bit, especially the potty-training years. He never really got the hang of that, although I think a lot of that time was solely about tormenting my mother. When he was a toddler he had trained himself to hang on to everything until she took him off the potty and dressed him again, it was his little game. Subsequently, now that he was older he was having a hard time retraining his bowels. Nothing ever happened when he sat on the toilet, he would sit there for ages then give up and get on with whatever he was doing only to get a surprise a few minutes later. He knew what screaming and swearing would occur if he told my mother so after the first few times he stopped telling her.

Instead he started hiding the evidence, he would take off his Donald Duck underpants which still contained said evidence. Then he would roll them up and hide them in his chest of drawers before getting on with his life. It never occurred to him to empty them down the loo and give them a quick rinse under the tap, or even throw them in the dustbin.

This would happen about twice a week so you can imagine the aroma coming from his bedroom after a few days. My mother was like a sniffer dog, rooting around his bedroom following the smell. When she found the evidence she would go nuts, screaming and shouting at him while waving the offending knickers under his nose. How would she ever live it down if anyone ever found out what a dirty little animal she had raised, how would she be able to hold her head up in the street? She didn't realise most of the street already knew anyway because she was broadcasting it to them through the window. My brother didn't care, by now he had picked up my parent's habit of rewriting his life. In his mind, once he had stashed his little package it disappeared, it simply didn't exist anymore.

This must have been the reason that he never got any better at hiding it from her, he always picked the same spot to hide the offending underpants. On top of that he never even thought to open his window. I don't know what people thought when they came to our house in the middle of summer. If they arrived before my mother had made her regular discovery they didn't stick around for long. My mother couldn't see her that visitors were going green and gagging because she too had erased the whole thing from her mind. It just wasn't happening and that was that. She took to carrying a can of air freshener in her pinny at all times though during his (as she put it) dirty, disgusting year. I don't think even her inner editing could completely obliterate the smell.

Now that I was twelve, my mother decided it was time I learned about periods. Obviously, she wasn't going to tell me anything herself so she sent away for a booklet from a sanitary towel firm. When I was younger I had come across the odd box of sanitary towels hidden away in my mother's cupboard a few times. They were huge thick things with big loops at both ends and I couldn't figure out what they were. I asked my mother once what they were but she just slapped me round the head with one and told me to mind my own business. The next time I dared to ask she told me they were bandages although when my dad twisted his ankle the bandage he had on looked nothing like that.

Anyway, when the booklet came she lobbed it in my direction and told me to read it carefully, it would explain everything about being a woman. I thought she meant it would explain why she was so weird, after all she was the woman, not me.

Closer inspection however showed lots of diagrams of body bits with strange names, it was far from straightforward. Looking back now I think it must have been written by a man. I turned it this way and that for a while to try and work out what I was looking at then I looked at the written bits. It was all about fertilising eggs and not washing your hair at that certain time of the month, it was quite boring. I ended up more confused after reading it than I had been before. I showed it to Melanie who was as clueless as I was about the whole growing up thing. She had an older sister remember but she never told us much, just that we'd understand things when we were older. I had been hearing that all my life and I was still none the wiser. It was ridiculous really, we were almost teenagers and we had no idea about anything. Melanie was still under the impression that babies came out of your belly button, and her mother and father were both nurses.

We read through the booklet again but it was hard reading. At the back of the book were a few pages of exercises that could be done at that 'certain' time of the month to make you feel better. We didn't know if this was the proper time of the month but we had nothing better to do so off we went into the garden and did a few jumping jacks and lunges. Afterwards I reminded Melanie not to wash her hair. Then we went off to eat some chocolate as it said in the book we may find it beneficial if we felt tired. After all that exercise we thought that sounded like a good idea.

Were we in for a rude awakening.

That summer when I was twelve was a special time for me because I got my first boyfriend. His name was Adrian and he lived further up the street from me. We would hang around in the same gang and split into two teams to play football in the garages behind the houses.

I don't remember ever speaking to him but one day his friend asked my friend if I would be Adrian's girlfriend. This sounded quite exciting to me so I said ok and we ended up going out for the next two weeks. For all of those two weeks we never actually spoke to each other or even looked at each other. Actually, I didn't even like him that much but I liked the idea of telling people I had a boyfriend.

Eventually, I decided I wasn't ready for a serious relationship and so I told my friend to tell his friend to tell Adrian I didn't want to go out with him anymore. I don't know how he took the news as we never spoke but I don't think he was too upset. I'm not sure he even knew he was going out with me anyway.

I had enough to worry about anyway with 'big school' coming up, I had no time for distractions.

It was while I was in my last year at junior school that I experienced my last ever act of violence from a teacher. Once at high school all that nonsense stopped, probably because half the kids were bigger than the teachers. In fact in my last year there one of the teachers was beaten up by a pupil while another locked himself in the paper cupboard (it wasn't made of paper, it was where paper was kept) to escape a good hiding.

Anyway, as was the norm this time once again it was nothing to do with me. We were in the middle of a history lesson with Miss Winchester, she was a very small, manly sort of a woman who liked to perch on her desk trying to look cool. We were spread out around the classroom in groups of six or eight and our desks were pushed together. I was sitting with my back to Miss Winchester opposite another girl and I was facing the window. Mid lesson she said she could hear someone whispering and demanded that the culprit own up. I was sitting there thinking that nobody was daft enough to own up to it when she pounced. I must say, she was very light on her feet because the first I knew of anything was when the pain shot through my spine and she screeched in my ear:

"It's You Girl."

Once more I was getting the blame when I hadn't even opened my mouth. She shoved me so hard in the back that the force of it sent the other desks flying, I hit the desk ribs first and ended up wedged tight between my chair and the desk. She demanded that I tell her what was so interesting that I couldn't wait until playtime to talk about it. I would have told her that it wasn't me but I was too busy trying to breathe and extract my desk lid from my intestines at the same time. I must say, for a small woman she was exceedingly strong.

The rest of the class sat in shock, not daring to move a muscle in case she started on them. No doubt the whisperer was thanking their lucky stars that she'd blamed me instead. She gave me another couple of digs in the back for good measure and then told me to put the desks back together and keep my mouth shut in future

The next day my ribs and my back were black and blue and I had the imprint of the desk on my stomach. Despite this it never crossed my mind to tell my parents, I would have been far more mortified if my mother had come into school shouting the odds. I don't think I ever told them what had happened even after I was grown up.

If time travel is ever invented in my lifetime I think that's the first place in my past I would go back to. I would be ready this time though so when she made her move I would jump out of the way before she hit me and watch smugly as she followed my desk straight out of the window and down onto the pavement two storeys below.

Unfortunately, that wasn't my last run in with Miss Winchester and once again (you've guessed it) I got the blame again for something someone else had done. I'm not fibbing here, it's really true that everything I ever got in trouble for (apart from the Wise Man fiasco in primary school) was never my fault, I must have just had a guilty expression for those early years.

Anyway, it was a few months after the last incident and the memory had faded along with my bruises. I had been home for my dinner and came back to find a note doing the rounds of our class, it was supposedly from me and it was to a boy in our class saying I wanted to have a look down his trousers (oh the humour). I knew which girl had written it so just rolled my eyes and ignored it and started getting ready for maths. Just as the lesson was beginning someone came in with a message that Miss Winchester wanted to see me in her office, she had recently been promoted to deputy head and was on even more of a power trip than usual.

With a sinking heart I headed off to see what she wanted with me. I knew whatever it was it would be bad news, she wasn't calling me in for tea and biscuits. I got there, knocked on the door and waited for her to shout me in. Once inside I saw her sitting at her desk, she looked up and waved a note at me,

"Would you mind explaining why you are passing filth like this around my school?" she snapped.

Oh god, she had the note from class that was supposed to be from me. I wouldn't have called it filth though, compared to most of the conversations in our class nowadays it was very tame, I was certainly no David Townsend.

I tried to explain to her that I hadn't written it, someone else had signed my name. I knew who it was but I didn't say, I was no grass, I'd seen the Sweeney. She asked me to explain why it was in my handwriting then and waved it under my nose. It looked nothing like my writing and the word trousers wasn't even spelt right. She wouldn't pay any attention to my protests though and said she was going to get to the bottom of it. She threw a pile of exercise books at me, all from our class and told me to pick out all the ones that looked like the writing in the note. I obliged, picking out a few that resembled the writing, I thought I'd better include my own even though it looked nothing like it. I didn't want to get her back up even more. When I'd finished, I handed her the suspect pile and she went through them one by one, throwing each one aside as soon as she'd glanced at it.

"Not that one, not that one, not that one."

When she came to mine she threw that onto the pile as well, I pointed out that she had dismissed my writing but that only made her madder.

She puffed out her skinny, manly chest and told me to get out, that this was far from over and she was going to prove that I was the culprit. Blimey, she was in the wrong job here, she should have been at Scotland Yard.

I went back to my maths lesson and got caught up on what I'd missed. Ten minutes later the door opened and in stalked Miss Winchester. What now? Was she going to cart me off again and shine a bright light into my eyes until she forced me to admit I was the phantom writer? Maybe she was she going to try a bit of torture this time? To my surprise, she ignored me and went over to speak to the maths teacher. They did a bit of whispering together while I held my breath and waited for whatever was to come.

Miss Winchester turned to the class and announced that we were about to have a surprise history spelling test (this was beyond belief now). Everyone was most confused, why were we having a history test in the middle of maths, and why a spelling test, surely that was for our English lesson? Meanwhile the maths teacher was handing out bits of paper to the class.

With no further explanation, Miss Winchester perched her bony arse on the desk and away we went.

"First word" she announced " is Cromwell."

We all wrote down the word and waited for the next one.

"Roundhead" she said.

These words were from the period in history that we had been learning about. She followed up with a few more historical words and then came out with:

"Trousers."

Oh my god, if this wasn't so awful it would be funny. I duly obliged and wrote down 'trousers' clearly, making sure I spelt it absolutely correctly. After a few more words from our history lessons she collected up the papers and stalked off looking very pleased with herself, now she would have her proof. She went off back to her office leaving our class looking at each other, thoroughly confused and not sure what had just happened.

And that was that. Nothing came of it, it was never mentioned again and the Miss Sodding Marple of the History Department carried on as if nothing had ever happened. She treat me exactly the same as she had before and I never even got an apology, what a liberty. The real culprit must have spelt the offending word correctly this time because they were never carted off for interrogation as I had been. On top of that we never did get the results of our spelling test.

That was the last time I remember ever being in trouble at school. A few weeks later the end of term rolled around and that was that, my days at junior school had come to an end. When the summer holidays were over I would be in senior school, a few months after that I would be a teenager. It was a scary thought but even more scary was the fact that three short years after that school would be over completely. I would be out on my own in the big bad world, that thought was completely terrifying.

What would I do for a job?

What would I do with my life?

What would fate have in store for me and the lunatics I called my family?

If only I'd known.

Still, that's another story.

THE END

Printed in Poland
by Amazon Fulfillment
Poland Sp. z o.o., Wrocław

53897833R00129